Mediterra

Recipes from the islands and
shores of the Mediterranean

Mediterra
Ben Tish

Photography by
Kris Kirkham

BLOOMSBURY ABSOLUTE
LONDON · OXFORD · NEW YORK · NEW DELHI · SYDNEY

Designer
Peter Moffat
for Jon Croft Editions

Photographer
Kris Kirkham

Photographer's Assistants
Rosie Alsop, Amy Grover,
Alexis Ko and Sam Milton

Prop Stylist
Davina Perkins

Prop Stylist's Assistant
Stevie Taylor

Food Stylists
Ben Tish with Helen Gurnett,
Richard Sandiford and
Neradah Hartnett

Copyeditor
Beverly Le Blanc

Proofreader
Rachel Malig

Indexer
Zoe Ross

BLOOMSBURY ABSOLUTE
Bloomsbury Publishing Plc
50 Bedford Square, London, WC1B 3DP, UK
29 Earlsfort Terrace, Dublin 2, Ireland

BLOOMSBURY, BLOOMSBURY ABSOLUTE
and the Diana logo and the Absolute Press logo are
trademarks of Bloomsbury Publishing Plc

First published in Great Britain 2024

A catalogue record for this book is available from the British Library

Library of Congress Cataloguing-in-Publication data has been applied for

HB 9781526661135
ePub 9781526661128
ePDF 9781526661142

10 9 8 7 6 5 4 3 2 1

Printed in China by C&C Offset Printing Co., Ltd.

MIX
Paper | Supporting
responsible forestry
FSC® C008047

To find out more about our authors and books visit
www.bloomsbury.com and sign up for our newsletters.

Introduction

Each and every country around the Mediterranean has its own food style and unique dishes, and while geography and cultures differ, east to west, Christian to Muslim, there is a commonality that runs through them all, bringing the region together in one glorious whole: the hot summers and dry winters, coastal briny winds, alfresco eating, vibrant street foods, hectic food markets, a relaxed way of life where meal times are sacrosanct. This is the true Mediterranean.

Over the centuries, the seaports of the Mediterranean welcomed a steady flow of visitors and traders from all over the world who helped to create a food culture unlike anywhere else. A food culture that is a mix of frugality borne out of poverty and self-preservation, intertwined with elements of luxury and sophistication introduced by many but in particular the conquering rulers of past centuries – the Arabs, Romans and Ottomans.

The common thread of Mediterranean cooking is the instinctive need to use the best seasonal and regional ingredients from land and sea, prepared with love and care in the simplest of ways. This is a cuisine of the sun. A cuisine of fragrance and flavour: olive oil, fresh herbs, ripe seasonal tomatoes, juicy stone fruits and oozy figs, sizzling garlic, crushed spices aromatic from roasting, the perfumed zest of orange, lemon and bergamot, smoky grilled meats served with flatbreads to mop up the juices, and the freshest fish grilled over hot coals. This is the food that I love.

Mediterranean Passion

My life changed 20 years ago when a chance opportunity
arose to help at the opening of a new Italian restaurant.
Though I'd been in love with the food of the Mediterranean
for most of my culinary career, my early years had been spent
working in and around London at various high-end, classical,
Michelin-starred restaurants. And while I enjoyed my time
in these sacred places, I never really felt a connection with
the formal French fare that was being cooked and served.
Yes, we cooked delicious, highly crafted and labour-intensive
food but never really with soul or passion. At that time in the
grand kitchens of London there was little understanding of
provenance and seasonality. We would be cooking asparagus
and strawberries at Christmas without a second thought other
than how to make it look as pretty as possible.

So, when I walked in through the doors of Al Duca that
day in 2000 it was as if the lights had been turned on for
the very first time. The all-southern Italian team were
completely focused on the food and authenticity. Each
morning the produce arriving at the kitchen was lovingly
checked, fondled and caressed. Beautiful knobbly, leafy
lemons were sniffed and the scent inhaled, as were a variety
of misshapen courgettes, still caked with earth. Spiky, fresh
young artichokes glistening with dew flown in from Sardinia
that morning and only available for 6 weeks a year were like
nothing I'd seen before. I could even smell the tomatoes
before they had arrived in the kitchen. There were specific
tomatoes for specific disciplines: San Marzano for sauces,
datterini and plum vine for salads, Carmona for roasting. I
loved the detail and I loved that it all made culinary sense.
The food we put on the plate was delicious, vibrant, colourful
and fresh.

At first, I was a little nervous about the simplicity of it all, having been brought up in a tradition of over-complicating dishes, constantly labouring over trying to balance towers of ingredients and then carefully having to place herbs and garnishes on top, just so. Here at Al Duca there were just two or three things on the plate, always in season and at their prime and of only the very best quality.

It was also the first time I had used a charcoal grill in a restaurant environment. Meat, fish and vegetables were grilled to give a deliciously smoky char and crust, enhancing the natural flavours. We cooked fish on the bone, basted with extra virgin olive oil, lemon juice and fresh herbs.

We grilled stone fruits, plums and peaches, brushed with honey to accompany a simple clean panna cotta. Nothing more, nothing less.

Butter was noticeably absent, replaced with copious amounts of fruity extra virgin olive oil – we used gallons of it both in cooking and dressings.

The enthusiasm for ingredients in the kitchen was infectious and it was there that I started to learn about the importance of seasonality. I was working hand in hand with a team who had an inherent love and passion for cooking the food of their Mediterranean heritage. I was hooked.

A year later I was made head chef. I began travelling to southern Italy, visiting Calabria, Puglia, Sardinia and Sicily as often as I could to soak up the culture, discover regional recipes, learn about new ingredients and find new producers.

My whole outlook on food had changed radically and I had become motivated and passionate about what I put on the plate. At Al Duca I had found my calling and I was hungry to explore other Mediterranean countries and their food cultures.

In 2004 I left Al Duca and joined Salt Yard as head chef. Salt Yard was a new restaurant that championed both Mediterranean food and also a more relaxed, social way of dining. We were cooking food from Spain, the main focus of the menu, Italy, North Africa and the Maghreb, Greece and most everything in between. I travelled extensively, exploring and researching. Spain and its islands were my hotspot for a while – Andalucía, Murcia, Valencia, Catalonia and the Balearic islands – submerging myself in the way of life. I fell in love with the incredible food markets: vegetables so big and bright that they startle you, seafood so fresh and often alive, varieties I'd never seen before, many almost alien-like. I fell in love with the tapas bars, happily eating my way around town; one dish here, two dishes and a glass or two of sherry there. The bars all specializing in something specific – anchovies, mushrooms, foie gras, tomatoes, peppers. And it was in Spain that I fell in love with cooking over open fire. Charcoal grills are commonplace in the restaurants and homes of Spain, as indeed they are in many parts of the Mediterranean. Anything cooked over charcoal tastes fantastic! Fish, meat, fruit and vegetables all benefit from the lick of smoke enhanced by dry olive or fig branches thrown onto the flames.

With Salt Yard successfully established, I opened Ember Yard in 2012, a Mediterranean grill restaurant.

While exploring the region of Andalucía I had become more and more interested in the Moors, their history and their influence on the food culture. This interest inspired my travels to North Africa's Mediterranean coast and to Morocco, Algeria and Tunisia in particular to discover the differences and similarities between the food of Mediterranean Andalucía and Mediterranean North Africa. Dishes such as the Spanish *escalivada* and Moroccan *mechouia* (page 223) are prepared in very similar ways but with the introduction of local spices such as caraway. For religious and cultural reasons pork is not eaten and lamb takes centre stage. Tomatoes, lemons and olive oil are as prevalent as they are in the west, along with the cooking techniques such as grilling fish and meat over charcoal, deep frying in olive oil and the use of local fresh herbs to add flavouring to dishes.

By chance, a wine trip with a supplier took me on a tour of Istria to Croatia and Slovenia which border Italy. Two countries that not everyone knows have Mediterranean coastlines. The food was beguiling – a subtle blend of northern Italian staples and heartiness with an undercurrent of Mediterranean warmth and vibrancy. Dishes such as steamed mussels with wine, dried chilli and thyme (page 87) and the Croatian-style polenta (Zganci, page 94) cooked with handfuls of fresh Mediterranean herbs and salty sheep's cheese, along with plentiful amounts of olive oil for cooking and flavouring typify the mouth-watering cuisine. And the wine is fabulous too.

My interest by now had become focused on Sicily and the very southern regions of Italy, such as Sardinia, Puglia and Calabria. And so in 2019 I opened a restaurant called Norma, named after Sicily's signature dish, Pasta alla Norma, and wrote a love letter to Sicily in the form of a book – *Sicilia*. Sicily still holds a special place in my heart and I still have many areas of the island to explore.

The eastern coastline of the Mediterranean was first introduced to me by my long-time friend Kevin Gould, a passionate foodie and advocate of this corner of the Mediterranean. Turkey and further east, to Syria, Israel, Palestine and Lebanon, have now become regular destinations for me and my wife, Nykeeta. We have spent many happy weeks exploring this part of the world, immersing ourselves in the amazing food culture. Grilled or baked smoky flatbreads and exciting, multi-coloured and multi-textured salads are always a favourite. My pear, radish and watercress salad on page 158 is a riot of flavour for which I've cherry-picked my fondest food memories to pile into a single salad. I love the exotic and heavy spicing reminiscent of North Africa, the fragrant flower waters, the highly spiced slow-cooked meat (see my lamb version on page 130) or small cuts just flash grilled over coals and, of course, the rich, creamy desserts with fresh yoghurt, labneh and honey-drenched pastries. I've been really inspired by my culinary experiences in the region and have relished playing with flavours and ingredients prominent in the area to create original dishes.

My most recent Mediterranean adventures have been spent around the Greek islands. Like so many before me I have become utterly enchanted by the blue upon blue of the seas, the rugged *terroir* and the charming locals. The food is incredibly simple and delicious: smoky grilled lamb and chicken, buttery flatbreads, sharp lemony dips, creamy yoghurt, simple grilled fishes, swathes of mint and dill, bulging figs and plump olives like no other. Oh, and the olive oil – I think it to be the world's best.

With all this travelling and experience I decided to create and cook a menu of pan-Mediterranean food at a new restaurant at the Princess Royal, which I opened in 2022. The Princess Royal is a beautiful London pub with a walled garden in London's Notting Hill. A London pub may seem unlikely for a Mediterranean offering, but it seems to work. I devised dishes that were inspired by my travels around the Mediterranean, both new creations and old classics given a twist. Vibrant, delicious, easy and convivial.

The Book

Originally this book had a much smaller scope. It was to focus on the Mediterranean countries that we all know so well. But a pivotal call to change came from my publisher, Jon Croft, who said that if I was going to write a book about this region's cuisine then, I should do it justice and cover the majority of the Mediterranean basin. Mediterranean books have been written before but covering only a handful of the countries. I had a wealth of experience to share, having covered most of the Mediterranean myself. A wise call from Jon, and although he doubled my workload overnight, the book has been a joy to put together. It has been fascinating to compare and connect the recipes that run along the shoreline of the Mediterranean.

The recipes in this book are dishes I cook at home and at work. They are dishes I love to share with friends, family and customers alike. The recipe inspiration for *Mediterra* spans my personal experience of the Mediterranean and most of the basin – across Europe, North Africa and the eastern shores.

I've divided the book geographically, firstly into the main areas – the northern, eastern and southern shores and the islands – and then each of these by country. It may surprise you that some of these countries are part of the Mediterranean, but reading the recipes you'll see the thread that runs through and links them together.

The recipes are full of passion, colour and flavour, simple and accessible, and will transport you to the sun-soaked shores of the Mediterranean basin. There are dishes inspired by the classics and dishes inspired simply by a holiday or an ingredient. I try to be seasonal as it is better tasting, more economical and more environmentally friendly. Most of the dishes are quick and can be made for a midweek dinner, while others will require a bit more time and planning – perfect for a weekend project.

I love sharing food, not just when in the restaurant cooking and seeing people enjoying it, but also around the family table. Sharing and social eating and drinking is so much more than the sum of its parts. Trying many different flavours without restriction is a joy. The heartbeat of conviviality opens up conversation and friendships are formed and strengthened.

So, if I have a message it is to not only cook like a Mediterranean, but to also eat like a Mediterranean: take time, invite friends and family, pour a glass of wine and lay the table.

northern shores

Spain
France
Italy
Slovenia
Croatia
Greece

Fondly remembered childhood travels and exciting adult food adventures – the northern shores of the Mediterranean is where my love of all things Mediterranean began. Here are just a few of my favourite northern shore memories and highlights, should you find yourself in this part of the world with time to explore.

Panisse in Nice

My childhood holidays were spent trekking on food safaris around the south of France with my parents and their friends, soaking up the heady scents of garlic and thyme. Whether eating fruit-studded clafoutis at small neighbourhood bistros or crisp fried *panisses* with melted cheese on the street corners of Nice, I knew this was a world in which I belonged.

Later in life, my trips with friends to Spain, Italy and Greece were always broken up with deep searches for local foods. These trips instilled a life-long love of pasta, rice, the freshest grilled seafood that the sea has to offer and meats of all shapes and varieties, marinated with herbs and vinegar.

I have a sweet tooth! My first proper tiramisu in Italy set me off on a still unfinished journey to find and make the ultimate version. The recipe on page 69 gets close, but I'm not quite there yet.

Culinary surprises in Istria

When I was running a small collection of Mediterranean restaurants in London, I would spend time travelling to the region, soaking up the culture and discovering new dishes, ingredients and producers.

It was then, when possibilities and ambition were fuelled by accessibility, that I fell upon the joys of Croatia and Slovenia. Just across the Adriatic from Italy's east coast and making up part of the triumvirate of Istria, both countries are gently touched by Italy's food culture, while proudly displaying their own distinct culinary identities. The two countries endorse a hearty approach to the table, celebrating beans, polenta, grains and potatoes as a base for dishes, while also using the Mediterranean staples of olive oil, fresh herbs, garlic and bay to sing the lighter food songs of the Mediterranean.

Island hopping

In recent years, I've fallen deeply in love with the Greek islands. I relish the simplicity of the life and the food.

My wife, Nykeeta, and I like to island hop, staying in small hotels or villas, visiting tavernas or wandering the food markets, basking in the warmth of the people, the climate, the culture and the glorious simplicity of the exquisite food.

Richly flavoured olive oil, irresistible taverna-fried chips with grilled kebabs, feta-topped salads, lemon-stuffed sea bream or sea bass cooked over wood or charcoal, grilled squid simply seasoned with sea salt, olive oil and a sprinkling of chilli flakes … my favourite foods in favourite places.

Slow-cooked lamb in wood ovens

The outdoor wood oven is almost as common in Greece as the indoor oven is in the United Kingdom. And yes, it really is a wonderful thing, producing deliciously flavoured foods in glorious surroundings.

Slow roasting a shoulder of lamb, rubbed with dried oregano, oil and vinegar, for three to four hours on a Greek island getaway in an outdoor wood oven is hard to beat.

The romance of the setting adds immeasurably to the irresistible wafts of sweet smoke and herbs emanating from the melting lamb fat. I adore it. My very favourite food experience? Quite possibly!

Ajo Blanco
chilled almond and garlic soup

I've often written of my love for this wonderful chilled Andalusian soup, a dish created by the Arabs during the Middle Ages on their rolling conquest of Spain and Southern Europe. Traditionally, this was made up of nothing more than the three key ingredients of almond, garlic and bread, with perhaps just a splash of sherry vinegar.

The soup still features on Andalusian restaurant menus and is prepared by local home cooks in the hot summer months. Here is my most recent favourite version of this glorious soup.

Serves 4–6

50g day-old white bread with crusts removed and ripped into small pieces
275g blanched almonds
300–400ml ice-cold water
2 small garlic cloves, chopped
50ml extra virgin olive oil, plus extra to garnish
1½ tablespoons muscatel vinegar or white balsamic
sea salt and freshly ground black pepper

To garnish
75g seedless black grapes, halved lengthways and chilled
½ cucumber, peeled and finely chopped
a handful of dill fronds

Place the bread in a bowl and pour over a little cold water. Leave to soak for 15 minutes, or until very soft.

Meanwhile, place the almonds in a food processor and blitz until you have a fine powder, scraping down the side of the bowl, as necessary – the almonds will stick to the side. Pour in 200ml of the ice-cold water and blend until you have a loose paste. Add the garlic and continue blending for a further 2 minutes.

Squeeze the water out of the bread and add the bread to the almond paste along with the extra virgin olive oil and vinegar. Continue blending, slowly adding the remaining water until you have a consistency you like.

When the water is fully incorporated, season the *ajo blanco* with salt and pepper, then transfer to the fridge for at least 1 hour before serving.

To serve, pour into chilled bowls and garnish with the grapes, cucumber and dill, then drizzle with extra virgin olive oil.

Empanadillas
with roasted aubergine, sheep's cheese and walnuts

These lovely little pastry turnovers are a Spanish classic. This is my version inspired by a trip to Granada in southern Spain. Hitting the sherry bars one night we received a platter of *empanadillas* from the oven. I was drinking a bone-dry, ice-cold fino sherry and ate a sweet-salty, cheese-stuffed *empanadilla* drizzled with honey. The combination was other worldly. One of those on-holiday food moments you just have to try and recreate when you get back home.

My version incorporates fried aubergine, fresh mint and some crunchy walnuts for added flavour and texture.

Makes 12

500g plain white flour
a pinch of table salt
100g unsalted butter, melted
about 200ml water
2 tablespoons clear honey
  for drizzling

For the filling
olive oil
1 aubergine, cut into 1cm dice
200g soft sheep's milk cheese, such
  as ricotta
25g walnut halves, toasted
1 teaspoon dried chilli flakes
a handful of mint leaves,
  roughly chopped
sea salt and freshly ground black
  pepper

First make the pastry. Mix the flour and salt together in a bowl. Make a well in the centre and stir in the melted butter and water. Bring together with your hands, then tip out onto a work surface and knead until a soft, smooth dough forms. Roll the dough into a ball and transfer back to a bowl, cover and place in the fridge for an hour or so to rest.

Meanwhile, preheat the oven to 240°C/Fan 220°C/Gas Mark 9 with a baking sheet inside.

To make the filling, heat a good splash of olive oil in a large sauté pan over a medium heat. When it is hot, add the aubergine and fry, stirring, for 4–5 minutes until the aubergine is golden brown and tender. Use a slotted spoon to transfer the aubergine to a bowl and set aside to cool.

Stir the sheep's cheese into the aubergine, along with the walnuts, chilli flakes and mint, and season with salt and pepper.

Divide the pastry into 12 equal pieces and roll into smooth balls with your hands. Using a lightly floured rolling pin, roll each ball into a 12cm circle. Lay out and place one tablespoon of the filling mix just slightly off-centre of each. One by one, brush the edge with water, then fold the pastry over to cover the filling and pinch the edges together between your finger and thumb to ensure the pastry is fully sealed. Continue until all are filled.

Carefully transfer the *empanadillas* to the hot baking tray and bake for 25 minutes, or until golden brown and crisp. Transfer to a wire rack and leave to cool for 2–3 minutes, then drizzle with the honey and serve.

Slow-roast Potatoes
with green sauce

A wonderful dish that hails from Majorca, where potatoes are revered as much as meat or fish. Hot, salty, crispy caramelised potatoes finished with a fresh, vibrant, punchy green salsa full of fresh coriander and green chillies. Simple contrasting flavours make this dish sing. It's one of my favourite potato dishes, great on its own or served with grilled meats and fish. You need a starchy potato for this, and I like pink firs, but rattes or Charlottes are also good. The salt seems excessive, but it helps dry the potatoes and creates a delicious salty crust.

Serves 4;
the sauce makes about 200ml

500g pink fir or other waxy, dry
    variety (see introduction,
    above), scrubbed
100g sea salt, plus extra for sprinkling
olive oil

For the green sauce (mojo verde)
100ml extra virgin olive oil
20ml red wine vinegar
1 tablespoon fennel fronds
1 green chilli, deseeded
1 garlic clove
100g coriander sprigs
50g flat-leaf parsley sprigs
½ green pepper, halved, cored
    and deseeded
½ teaspoon ground cumin
sea salt and freshly ground black
    pepper

Place the potatoes in a large saucepan and cover by 3cm with cold water. Add the 100g sea salt and then bring the water to the boil, covered. Uncover the pan, lower the heat and leave the potatoes to simmer until they are just tender. Drain well, and when they are cool enough to handle, cut in half lengthways.

Meanwhile, preheat the oven to 190°C/Fan 170°C/Gas Mark 5.

To make the *mojo verde*, place all the ingredients in a blender and blitz until a coarse paste forms. Season to taste. Set aside until needed.

Pour a good layer of olive oil into a roasting tray. Add the potatoes and stir them around, then sprinkle with more salt. Roast for 35–40 minutes, tossing once or twice, until they are crisp and golden brown. Drain the potatoes on a tea towel and serve with the *mojo verde* spooned over the top.

Gazpachuelo
Malaga-style fish stew with aïoli

A delicious, distinctive and unique 'white' fish stew found in Malaga and the surrounding area. This is the coastal version – the inland version contains bread and eggs. I like to use three or four seafood varieties for this. The trick to success lies in the technique of emulsifying a rich fish stock with aïoli, basically a garlic-flavoured fresh mayonnaise.

Serves a hearty 4–5

200g Atlantic or tiger prawns
olive oil
a glass of dry white wine
350ml fish stock (fresh or
    homemade is best)
350g Desiree or other waxy potatoes,
    peeled and roughly diced
3 fresh bay leaves
1 cinnamon stick
leaves picked from 5 fresh
    thyme sprigs
peeled zest of 1 unwaxed orange
200g white fish, such as hake or
    cod, unskinned and cut into
    bite-sized pieces
150g fresh mussels, debearded, if
    necessary, and washed in cold
    water; discard any that do not snap
    shut when tapped
100g fresh squid, rinsed, cleaned
    and sliced into rings (see page 32
    or ask a fishmonger to do this)
a handful of dill or fennel fronds,
    to serve
sea salt and freshly ground black
    pepper

For the aïoli
2 garlic cloves, crushed
2 large free-range egg yolks, at
    room temperature
250ml extra virgin olive oil
½ lemon

First make the stock base. Shell the prawns and remove the heads. Heat a good splash of oil in a saucepan over a medium-high heat. Add the prawn heads and shells. Stir for 5 minutes, pressing down with the back of a spoon to break up and expose more surface area and release flavour. Add the wine and leave it to bubble to evaporate, then add the stock. Simmer for 15 minutes, then turn off the heat and strain the stock, pressing down to release any remaining flavour.

Transfer the stock into the pan and bring back to a simmer. Add the potatoes, bay leaves, cinnamon, thyme leaves and orange zest, and cook slowly until the potatoes are just tender. Add the white fish, mussels and squid, and continue simmering for 5 minutes, or until the white fish flakes easily, the squid is tender and the mussels open – discard any mussels that remain closed. Turn off the heat and season with salt and pepper.

To make the aïoli, pound the garlic in a pestle and mortar and whisk in the eggs. Continue whisking, slowly adding the extra virgin olive oil in a thin stream until an emulsion forms – it's just like making mayonnaise. Season and squeeze in lemon juice to taste.

Stir a tablespoon of the warm stock into the aïoli, then follow with another spoonful of stock and repeat until you have a thin, cream-like consistency. Now whisk this mixture back into the remaining soup and bring back to a simmer – do not boil. Season again, if needed, and then divide among your bowls, topping with the dill or fennel fronds to serve.

Baked Crab
with oloroso and marjoram

This is a delicious way to prepare crab, inspired by the simple, robust cooking of the seaside towns and villages of Andalucía. The sherry's bitter-sweetness is a delicious foil for the rich crab. The marjoram, which is sprinkled on at the end of cooking, adds a wonderful aromatic waft as it hits the hot crab.

Traditionally, the crab would be baked and served in crab carapaces, making for a dramatic presentation. Fishmongers will be able to get them for you with some notice, and they can be reused.

Serves 6 as a starter

unsalted butter, softened, for
   greasing ramekins (optional)
6 crab shells, cleaned, for
   presentation (optional)
olive oil
1 onion, finely chopped
1 garlic clove, finely chopped
6 plum vine tomatoes, halved,
   deseeded and finely chopped
¼ teaspoon dried chilli flakes
¼ teaspoon smoked sweet paprika
75ml oloroso sherry
250g fresh handpicked white
   crab meat
200g fresh brown crab meat
leaves from ½ bunch of flat-leaf
   parsley, finely chopped
½ lemon
75g fresh breadcrumbs
a handful of fresh marjoram or
   oregano leaves, for sprinkling
sea salt and freshly ground black
   pepper

Preheat the oven to 220°C/Fan 200°C/Gas Mark 7. If you aren't using crab shells for presentation, butter six 150ml ramekins and place on a baking sheet; if using the shells, simply place them in a baking tray.

Heat a splash of olive oil in a large sauté pan over a medium heat. When it is hot, add the onion and fry, stirring, for 3–4 minutes until softened and golden. Add the garlic and stir for a further 1–2 minutes, then stir in the tomatoes, chilli flakes and paprika, and season well with salt and pepper. Simmer this for 5 minutes, stirring occasionally, or until the tomatoes are softened and jammy.

Pour in the sherry with a splash of water and boil for one minute. Stir in the white and brown crab meats, half the parsley and a squeeze of lemon juice. Adjust the salt and pepper, if necessary. Simmer for 1–2 minutes until the mixture is hot and the consistency is thick and rich.

Equally divide among the crab shells or ramekins, then top with the breadcrumbs, most of the remaining parsley and a drizzle of olive oil. Transfer the baking sheet to the oven and bake for 8–10 minutes until bubbling at the edges. Remove from the oven, sprinkle over the marjoram and remaining parsley and serve immediately.

Squid Stuffed with Sobrassada

I've always loved the combination of seafood and meat. This recipe comes from the Balearics, where the spicy, rich pork pâté *sobrassada* is omnipresent. Stuffing the squid with the pâté not only adds bags of flavour, but the fattiness also helps to keep the squid juicy and tender. A soft chorizo or 'nduja will work just as well. I think the honey offsets the spicy pork wonderfully.

Serves 4

olive oil
6 anchovy fillets in oil, drained and
    finely chopped
2 garlic cloves, finely chopped
1 large onion, finely chopped
½ teaspoon dried chilli flakes
4 plum tomatoes, cut into chunks
300g *sobrassada*, 'nduja or soft
    cooking chorizo
150g dried breadcrumbs
500g small whole fresh or defrosted
    squid bodies, rinsed and patted
    dry, with the tentacles cut off and
    reserved – if they need cleaning,
    follow the instructions on page 32
    or ask a fishmonger to do this
½ lemon
2 teaspoons clear honey
a splash of sherry vinegar
fresh oregano leaves for sprinkling
sea salt and freshly ground black
    pepper

Heat a splash of oil in a large sauté pan over a medium heat. When it is hot, add the anchovies and stir until they begin to dissolve. Add the garlic, onion and chilli flakes, and continue stirring until the onion is softened but without colour. Add the tomatoes and cook for a further 3 minutes, or until any liquid has evaporated. Lastly, stir in the *sobrassada* and breadcrumbs and cook slowly, stirring so nothing catches, for 5 minutes. Turn off the heat and leave to cool.

Carefully stuff the squid body cavities with the stuffing mix, filling each about three-quarters full, then secure the ends with wooden cocktail sticks.

Heat a good splash of oil in the washed and dried pan over a medium heat. When it is hot, add the stuffed squid and fry for 2–3 minutes on each side until caramelised. At the last minute add the tentacles to cook through. You might have to do this in batches, depending on the size of your pan. If so, keep the cooked squid hot in a low oven.

Turn off the heat (return any cooked squid to the pan) and season the pan juices well. Squeeze over the lemon juice, drizzle with honey and add the sherry vinegar, then leave to rest for 2 minutes. Serve the squid drizzled with the honey-lemon pan juices and oregano sprinkled over.

Arroz Negro
baked black rice with lemon, chilli and mint

The jet-black colouring of the rice comes from the addition of squid ink, which you can buy in sachets or jars from fishmongers. The ink not only adds colour, but also a wonderfully intense briny depth of flavour. The baking gives a caramelisation to the rice and concentrates the flavours of the seafood and stock.

Serves 4

400g fresh squid
200g clams, washed in cold water
olive oil
2 fresh bay leaves
2 garlic cloves, finely chopped
1 celery stick, finely chopped
1 onion, finely chopped
1 large fresh red chilli, deseeded and
  finely chopped
1 teaspoon sweet smoked paprika
300g paella rice
200ml dry sherry
4 x 4g sachets of squid ink
1.2 litres fish stock (fresh or
  homemade is best)
½ lemon
leaves from ½ bunch of mint,
  roughly chopped
leaves from ½ bunch of flat-leaf
  parsley, roughly chopped
sea salt and freshly ground black
  pepper

To clean the squid, rinse them well, then pat dry. Pull off the tentacles and head in one piece, then cut off the tentacles and set aside and discard the head. Pull out the hard beak from the centre of the body and discard. Use a small knife or even just your fingernails to peel off the skin. Slice the bodies into thin rings. Or ask a fishmonger to prepare the squid for you.

Preheat the oven to 180°C/Fan 160°C/Gas Mark 4. Discard any open clams that do not snap shut when sharply tapped.

Heat a splash of olive oil in a large flameproof casserole or deep ovenproof saucepan with a tight-fitting lid over a medium heat. When it is hot, add the bay leaves, garlic, celery, onion, chilli and paprika, and stir for 2–3 minutes until the onion is softened but without colour. Add the squid rings and tentacles and stir over a low heat for 5 minutes, or until they are cooked through and tender. Stir in the rice, making sure the grains are coated with oil. Season well with salt and pepper, pour in the sherry and leave to bubble until it is almost evaporated. Now stir in the squid ink and place the clams in the rice. Pour over the stock and bring to a simmer.

Cover the casserole and transfer to the oven for 15 minutes. Uncover and bake for a further 10 minutes or so until the stock has largely evaporated, and the rice is tender and starting to crisp a little on top. You want the consistency of a thick risotto. Add a splash of water if the rice looks too thick. Remove and discard any clams that have not opened.

When ready to serve, remove the casserole from the oven, squeeze in the lemon juice, stir in the chopped fresh herbs and check the seasoning. Serve at the table for people to help themselves.

Grilled Steaks on Toast
with caramelised onions, red peppers and melting cheese

This recipe is inspired by a fabulous restaurant in Seville called El Rinconcillo, which dates to the 15th century and serves traditional tapas and Andalusian classics. One of my favourites there is a grilled juicy steak on toast with melting cheese: the meaty steak juices and the olive oil soak into the warm bread to make the ultimate steak sandwich.

Here I've added some sweet onions and peppers, which make a nice contrast to the rich meat. A good melting cheese is important for gooeyness – Camembert works beautifully!

Serves 4

olive oil
2 large onions, thinly sliced
1 teaspoon light brown sugar
1 fresh bay leaf
1 large red pepper, cored, cut into 8 strips lengthways and deseeded
12 sage leaves
4 x 250g fillet steaks, each about 3cm thick, at room temperature
220g Camembert, rind removed and quartered
4 medium-thick slices white sourdough bread
smoked paprika
sea salt and freshly ground black pepper

Preheat the oven to 200°C/Fan 180°C/Gas Mark 6.

Heat a splash of oil in a saucepan over a low heat. When it is hot, add the onions, sugar and bay leaf, and season with salt and pepper. Cook steadily, stirring as you go, to soften and caramelise the onions. This will take a good while, probably 20 minutes to slowly turn the onions soft, sweet and a deep rich brown colour.

Meanwhile, place the pepper strips in a roasting tray, drizzle with olive oil and season. Transfer to the oven and roast until the peppers are tender and lightly blistered. Remove the tray from the oven and add the sage leaves to wilt in the residual heat.

After the onions have cooked for 10 minutes, heat a large ridged, cast-iron griddle pan or sauté pan over a high heat. Drizzle the steaks with olive oil and season them with salt and pepper. Add them to the pan and fry for 3 minutes on each side for medium-rare. Remove from the pan and place a piece of cheese on each steak while it's still hot so it starts to slowly melt. Leave to rest for a good 5 minutes.

Meanwhile, toast the bread. Top each slice with a mixture of onion and pepper, followed by a cheese-covered steak. Sprinkle with smoked paprika and a grind of pepper and serve.

Leche Fritta
fried milk with whipped cream and orange flower water

The origins of the *leche fritta* of Spain are hotly disputed. Murcia, Valencia, Andalucía and the Basque country all lay claim. I rather suspect, however, that the Arabs might have had a hand in creating this somewhere along the line. Essentially, this is a deep-fried, set custard with added spices and citrus. It should be served with something cold – a scoop of ice cream or a dollop of chilled whipped cream, spooned over the fritters immediately after frying so it melts on impact.

Serves 4–6

1 litre whole milk
1 vanilla pod, split lengthways
1 cinnamon stick
peeled zest of 1 unwaxed lemon
peeled zest of 1 unwaxed orange
3 large free-range egg yolks
130g cornflour
120g caster sugar
rapeseed oil for deep-frying

For the coating
100g cornflour
100g plain white flour
2 large free-range eggs, beaten
50g granulated sugar
1 teaspoon ground cinnamon

To serve
20g caster sugar
a few drops of orange flower water
100ml double cream, whipped
50ml orange blossom honey or
    clear honey

Line a 25 x 25cm baking tray with a piece of baking parchment large enough that it overhangs the edges, then set aside.

Pour 660ml of the milk into a saucepan over a medium heat with the vanilla pod, cinnamon stick and lemon and orange zests, and simmer until just hot. Turn off the heat and leave for 10 minutes to cool and infuse. Strain into a bowl and set aside. Scrape in the vanilla seeds, then discard the pod and other flavourings.

Whisk the egg yolks, cornflour and caster sugar together until light, fluffy and pale. Pour in the remaining milk and continue whisking until blended.

Transfer the infused milk back into the washed pan over a medium heat. Whisk in the cornflour mixture and slowly bring to a simmer. Lower the heat and whisk vigorously until the mixture thickens. Do not allow it to boil.

Pour the mixture into the baking tray and spread over the surface, into the edges, to create a layer about 2cm deep. Cover with cling film and set aside until cool. Transfer to the fridge for at least 3 hours, but you can leave for up to a day – ensure the custard is fully set before the next step.

Very gently use the overhanging lining paper to lift the set custard out of the tin, then cut it into pieces, about 5 x 3cm. Heat enough oil for deep-frying in a deep-fat fryer or heavy-based saucepan to 180°C. If you don't have a thermometer, a piece of bread dropped in the oil should sizzle and turn golden brown.

For the coating, mix the cornflour and plain flour together in a shallow tray. Beat the eggs in a separate tray and mix the sugar and cinnamon together in a third tray.

One by one, coat each piece of set custard on all sides in the cornflour mixture, then dredge through the eggs, tapping off the excess. Put it back into the cornflour mixture and tap off the excess.

When all the pieces have been coated, slide as many as will fit into the fryer and fry for 3–4 minutes, turning them as you go, until they are golden brown. Use a slotted spoon to remove them and immediately dredge them in the cinnamon-sugar mixture, evenly coating them on all sides. Set aside and keep hot until all the custard pieces are fried. Reheat the oil between batches.

To serve, stir the sugar and orange flower water into the whipped cream. Serve the fried bread pieces on plates and top each with a dollop of whipped cream and a good drizzle of blossom honey.

Burnt Cheesecake
with poached spice quince

Though this style of cheesecake is generally associated with the Basque country, most Spanish regions have a version, including Andalucía. It has the most incredible depth of flavour, is easy to make and a pure joy to eat. It is unique among cheesecakes in that it is crustless with a deep burnished, caramelly exterior. It's delicious on its own, but I like to pair it with spiced poached quinces, the sweet-sharpness of the fruit balancing the deep richness of the cheesecake.

Makes 6–8 slices

olive oil for greasing the tin
600g cream cheese
200g full-fat mascarpone
225g caster sugar
2 tablespoons plain white flour
200g soured cream
4 large free-range eggs
1 teaspoon vanilla extract
a pinch of table salt

For the poached quinces
200ml water
200ml sweet red wine
100g caster sugar
6 cloves
2 fresh bay leaves
2 star anise
1 cinnamon stick
2 quinces, peeled, quartered
    and cored

Preheat the oven to 240°C/Fan 220°C/Gas Mark 9 and grease a 20cm springform cake tin 10cm deep. Layer 2 large sheets of baking parchment, with the top sheet turned 45 degrees, so the corners form a star. Push the parchment into the tin, pressing it into the edge and ensuring the paper hangs over the side of the tin – roughly arranged is fine, as it gives the cheesecake a rustic feel. Set aside.

Whisk the cream cheese, mascarpone and sugar together in a mixing bowl until smooth and creamy. The sugar should be completely dissolved. Next add the flour, soured cream, eggs, vanilla and the salt, and whisk again until incorporated and the mixture is smooth. Pour it into the tin and give the tin a sharp knock on the work surface to remove any air bubbles.

Place the tin on a baking sheet and transfer to the oven. Bake the cheesecake for 30–35 minutes until it is just set and the top is dark and caramelised. A deep mahogany is what you're looking for – the bitterness contrasts with the rest of the rich cake. Transfer to a wire rack to cool, then chill for at least an hour before serving.

Meanwhile, prepare the quinces. Bring the water, wine and sugar to the boil with the cloves, bay leaves, star anise and cinnamon stick, stirring until the sugar dissolves. Add the quince pieces and reduce the heat so the liquid just simmers. Cover the pan and leave them to poach until they are just tender. Use a slotted spoon to remove the poached quinces and set them aside. Return the pan to the heat and bring the liquid to the boil. Continue boiling until it thickens and makes a syrup. Set aside and leave to cool, then return the quinces to the pan.

When you're ready to serve, unclip the tin and remove the side. Gently slide the cheesecake onto a serving platter. Use a wet knife to slice and serve with the poached quince and the poaching syrup.

My Aïoli

A traditional Mediterranean aïoli consists simply of an emulsion of pounded fresh garlic, salt and olive oil. My version is more akin to a garlic mayonnaise, creamier, softer and a little gentler on the garlic. I use it with many recipes – it works brilliantly as a cooling dip for fried seafood or to add a punchy richness to grilled fish and meat.

Once you've mastered the recipe you can add flavours of your choice, such as grain or Dijon mustard, ground almonds, chopped herbs or orange juice or zest.

Makes about 200ml

1 large free-range egg yolk
1 garlic clove, very finely chopped
1 small teaspoon Dijon mustard
200ml extra virgin olive oil
lemon juice
white wine vinegar, such as
    chardonnay
salt and freshly ground black pepper

Place the egg yolk in a bowl with the garlic and mustard and whisk together. Continue whisking and slowly add the oil to emulsify with the yolk. As the oil is incorporated into the yolk, you can speed up the process. When all the oil has been added, season with salt and pepper and add lemon juice and vinegar to taste. This will keep in a covered container in the fridge for up to 3 days.

Panisse
chickpea chips with sage and parmesan

The original *panisse* was created in the Italian region of Liguria, from where it steadily worked its way down and along the coast to Nice and Marseille in southern France.

I'm a great lover of this humble fried street food made with chickpea flour (gram flour), water, salt, olive oil and sometimes nuts. It is served in various ways depending on location and tradition. In my book *Sicilia*, I have a recipe for the golden and crispy Palermo version. This Nice version is a little fatter and wobblier on the inside. It is the perfect snack to accompany a cold apéritif.

Serves 4

olive oil
120g chickpea flour (gram
    flour), sifted
500ml cold water
2 tablespoons extra virgin olive oil
a handful of sage leaves
finely grated Parmesan
    cheese (optional)
4 lemon wedges, to serve
sea salt and freshly ground black
    pepper

Lightly grease a baking tray about 23 x 23cm with olive oil and set aside.

Place the chickpea flour into a saucepan and whisk in the water and then the extra virgin olive oil. Season well. Place the pan over a medium-low heat and stir for about 20 minutes until the mixture is thick and relatively smooth. Now either blend the mix with a hand mixer or transfer to a blender and buzz for a minute or two until nice and smooth. Return the batter to the pan and stir over a medium heat for a further 5 minutes.

Pour the batter into the baking tray, smooth the top and leave to set. You want the depth to be about 1cm and the top as smooth as you can make it, so it's best to use a wet metal spatula. Cover with a sheet of baking parchment, pressing it on the surface, so a skin doesn't form. Transfer to the fridge and leave for at least 4 hours or up to 24 hours.

Remove the set batter from the fridge, invert it onto a chopping board and cut into thick, fat chips.

Pour a good 1–1.5cm olive oil into a wide sauté pan over a medium heat. When it is 180°C, carefully transfer to the oil as many *panisses* as will fit without overcrowding the pan and fry until crisp and golden on all sides. You will probably have to do this in batches, so keep the fried ones warm in a low oven until they are all cooked. When all are fried, add the sage leaves to the oil and fry until they are crisp.

Transfer everything to kitchen paper to drain. Sprinkle with sea salt and Parmesan, if using, and serve with lemon wedges for squeezing over.

Provençal Soup
with young spinach, courgettes and white beans

This soup from the south of France is both hearty and vibrant, with aromas of herbs and garlic and glistening with pools of yellow-golden olive oil. It's the quintessential Mediterranean recipe, not at all dissimilar to the Italian summer minestrone of Liguria and Genoa. You get an instant hit of the garlic aroma as the *pistou* hits the hot soup. This is what elevates it above so many other vegetable soups.

Serves 4 or 5

olive oil
2 garlic cloves, sliced
1 large onion, finely chopped
2 fresh bay leaves
2 fresh thyme sprigs
50g new potatoes, scrubbed and cut
   into 0.5cm dice
2 courgettes, quartered lengthways
   and diced
1 plum tomato, roughly chopped
200g tinned white coco or cannellini
   beans, rinsed
30g dried pasta, such as spaghetti
   broken into bite-sized pieces,
   or ditalini
a good handful of baby spinach
   leaves, roughly chopped
100g frozen broad beans, defrosted
   and grey 'jackets' removed
extra virgin olive oil
sea salt and freshly ground black
   pepper

For the pistou
4 large garlic cloves, peeled
½ bunch of basil
50ml extra virgin olive oil
15g Parmesan cheese, finely grated

First make the *pistou*. Using a pestle and mortar, pound the garlic to a paste with a pinch of salt. Add the basil and a splash of extra virgin olive oil and continue pounding to make a green paste. Now stir in the remaining oil and Parmesan. Set aside.

To make the soup, heat a large splash of olive oil in a large saucepan over a low-medium heat. When it is hot, add the garlic, onion, bay leaves and thyme sprigs, and cook for 10–15 minutes until the onion is soft but without colour.

Add the potatoes and courgettes, season and cook for a further 20 minutes to soften, stirring as you go. Add the tomato and pour in cold water to just cover everything. Bring to the boil, then simmer for 10 minutes. Add the white beans and continue simmering for a further 5 minutes.

Stir in the pasta and boil for 10 minutes or so until it is al dente – the soup will become quite thick with the starch from the pasta. Stir in the spinach, broad beans and a good splash of extra virgin olive oil. Cook for no more than 2 minutes, or until the spinach wilts and the beans are hot. Season to taste and turn off the heat.

Divide the soup among serving bowls with the *pistou* served on the side, to be stirred into the soup just before eating.

Ratatouille

When made correctly, this classic Provençal dish epitomises the essence of Mediterranean cooking. The secret to success is to cook all the vegetables separately and then to carefully assemble them for a brief and gentle braise to allow the choir to sing together in perfect harmony. The ingredients should be of the very best quality.

After you've cooked the ratatouille, leave it to rest for at least an hour to allow the flavours to develop further. I always make a double or triple batch to keep in the fridge to eat with fish, meat, or on its own or as part of an antipasti or hors d'oeuvre course. It will keep for up to three days in the fridge.

Serves 4

olive oil
1 large white onion, thinly sliced
2 fresh bay leaves
½ bunch fresh thyme, tied together
2 long red Romano peppers, or 2 large
   red peppers
2 small aubergines, cut into
   bite-sized chunks
2 firm courgettes, cut into
   bite-sized chunks
3 garlic cloves, sliced
5 plum vine tomatoes, each cut
   into 6 wedges
extra virgin olive oil, to finish
a handful of basil leaves, to finish
sea salt and freshly ground black
   pepper

Heat a good splash of olive oil in a heavy-based saucepan with a lid over a medium heat. When it's hot, add the onions, bay leaves and thyme. Turn the heat to low, cover the pan and leave the onions to sweat for about 30 minutes, stirring occasionally to avoid them sticking, until they are meltingly soft but without colour. Remove the pan from the heat and set aside.

Meanwhile, preheat the oven to 240°C/Fan 220°C/ Gas Mark 9.

Rub the peppers with olive oil and roast for 15–20 minutes until they are soft and the skins start to blacken. Transfer the peppers to a bowl, cover with cling film and leave to steam – this makes it easy to peel off the skins.

Now, heat a large sauté pan over a medium heat with 2 good splashes of oil. When it is hot, add the aubergines to the pan, season and fry until they are softened and golden brown. You'll need to turn them a few times so they cook evenly. Add more oil as needed, as aubergines soak up the oil while cooking. Transfer to the pan with the cooked onions.

Use crumpled kitchen paper to wipe the sauté pan clean. Place over a medium heat with another splash of olive oil. When it is hot, add the courgettes, season and fry, turning occasionally, until they are softened and golden brown. Transfer to the pan along with the onions and aubergines.

Remove the peppers from the bowl, trim the ends, peel, halve and discard the seeds. Cut into rough strips and add to the pan with the other ingredients.

Finally, wipe the sauté pan clean again. Place over a medium heat and add more olive oil. When it is hot, add the garlic and tomato wedges, season and stir until the tomato wedges begin to break down and collapse a little and the garlic is golden and fragrant.

Transfer the tomatoes and garlic to the pan with the other vegetables, partially cover and place over a low heat. Cook slowly, stirring carefully once or twice, for about 30 minutes. The tomatoes will break down further, but you don't want them to turn to mush. I like to add extra virgin olive oil at this stage with the basil. Stir through and set aside for a good while. Serve warm or at room temperature.

Salmon Baked in Fig Leaves
with fennel fronds and orange zest

A Provence summer classic when there's an abundance of fig leaves on the trees just ahead of the fruit picking. Fig leaves are very versatile and can be used to envelop fish, lamb or pork, and they impart a fragrant fig flavour while keeping everything moist and juicy. You can even use fig leaves to infuse custards, soups and ice creams. They add a 'figgy' flavour, lighter and fresher than the actual fruit.

Serve this with some simply steamed new potatoes, aïoli (try my recipe on page 38 or buy a jar) and a bowl of ripe tomatoes.

Serves 4

8 large fig leaves, washed and
    kept damp
4 fillets organic or wild salmon, about
    200g each, skinned
extra virgin olive oil
grated zest and juice of ½ orange
a small handful of fennel fronds,
    fennel herb or dill fronds
sea salt

Preheat the oven to 200°C/Fan 180°C/Gas Mark 6.

Place 4 fig leaves on a baking sheet, then lay one salmon fillet on top of each. Drizzle each with oil, scatter over the orange zest and juice and small pieces of fennel fronds, and season with salt. Cover with the remaining fig leaves, folding the edges under the salmon to create a rough parcel. Insert a wooden cocktail stick in each parcel to secure.

Transfer the baking sheet to the oven and bake for 10–12 minutes until the flesh is just cooked through and flakes easily – the only way you can test this is to cut into one of the parcels. Immediately transfer the salmon parcels to a serving platter, still wrapped in the fig leaves for effect.

Roasted Chicken
with grapes, wine and rosemary

There's something so wonderfully comforting and therapeutic about the whole process of roasting a chicken. This exquisite Provençal version sets sweet roasted grapes and fragrantly aromatic rosemary as a backdrop to the salty chicken.

My friend Christophe, also vegetable supplier extraordinaire to my restaurants, hails from a small village just outside of Arles. He is forever proudly boasting that all the local households prepare an unbeatable version of this recipe when grapes from the harvest are abundant and in danger of going to waste. This is mostly his mum's recipe.

Serves 6

1 red onion, unpeeled and cut
   into quarters
1 garlic bulb, cut in half widthways
1 oven-ready, free-range chicken,
   about 1.8kg
olive oil
4 fresh rosemary sprigs
½ unwaxed lemon
700g seedless red or black grapes,
   ideally on their stalks
200ml dry red wine
300ml chicken stock (fresh or
   homemade is best)
sea salt and freshly ground black
   pepper

Preheat the oven to 220°C/Fan 200°C/Gas Mark 7.

Put the onion and one half of the garlic bulb in a deep roasting tin. Rub the chicken with olive oil, then season all over and inside the cavity with salt and pepper. Place one rosemary sprig, the lemon half and the remaining garlic bulb half in the cavity. Place the chicken on the onion and garlic and transfer the tin to the oven. Roast the chicken for 30 minutes, or until the skin has started to brown nicely and caramelise.

Reduce the temperature to 180°C/Fan 160°C/Gas Mark 4. Scatter around the grapes and remaining rosemary sprigs, and pour around the wine and half the stock. Continue roasting for a further 45 minutes, or until the chicken is cooked through – it should be crisp and golden on the outside and the juices should run clear when the thigh is pierced.

Transfer the chicken to a rimmed plate, cover with kitchen foil and leave to rest for 15 minutes. Do not turn off the oven.

Meanwhile, strain all the juices from the roasting tin into a saucepan and put the grapes back in the tin and return to the oven. Roast for a further 5 minutes, or until they are sticky and begin to caramelise.

Add the remaining stock to the saucepan and boil for 10 minutes, or until the juices have reduced and thickened. Serve the chicken with the sticky, sweet grapes and the sauce for pouring over at the table.

Rich Provençal-style Beef Daube
with cinnamon and orange

The ultimate Provençal beef stew. A magnificently rich and heady beef braise to warm up the coldest winter nights or the freshest spring days. Its origins lie in rural France, created by peasant farmers using a cheap meat that required a long cooking time in order to yield all the wonderful flavours. Traditionally this would be cooked slowly in an outdoor stove or clay oven, sometimes for as long as overnight.

Allow enough time to make the daube a day ahead so all the flavours blend. Serve with something plain and simple, such as mashed potatoes or buttered pasta.

Serves a very hearty 4 or 5

1 large celery stick
2 dried bay leaves
2 large flat-leaf parsley sprigs
2 large fresh thyme sprigs
800g piece of beef chuck, cut across
   the grain into 3mm slices
olive oil
150g unsmoked, free-range bacon,
   cut into short, chunky strips
3 onions, halved and thinly sliced
3 garlic cloves, thinly sliced
40g unsalted butter
30g plain white flour
400ml red wine, such as
   cabernet sauvignon
200ml beef stock (fresh or
   homemade is best)
400g tinned chopped tomatoes
250g carrots, peeled and cut into
   small chunky pieces
2 anchovy fillets in oil, drained
   and chopped
4 strips of peeled unwaxed
   orange zest
2 cinnamon sticks
60g unpitted black olives
salt and freshly ground black pepper

For the persillade, to garnish
a handful of flat-leaf parsley leaves,
   finely chopped
3 garlic cloves, finely chopped
extra virgin olive oil

First make a bouquet garni by cutting the celery stick in half lengthways, then sandwiching the herbs between the 2 pieces and tying everything into a tight bundle with kitchen string. Set aside.

Preheat the oven to 160°C/Fan 140°C/Gas Mark 3.

Meanwhile, pat the beef dry. Heat a splash of olive oil in a large flameproof casserole over a medium-high heat. When it is hot, add the beef, in batches, and fry to caramelise all over. Transfer each batch to a plate and season.

Add the bacon to the fat remaining in the casserole and fry until golden brown, then set aside with the beef.

Heat another splash of oil to the casserole, then add the onions and fry for 10–12 minutes until richly browned and slightly caramelised. Add the sliced garlic and fry for a further minute. Now add the butter and when it foams, stir in the flour and continue stirring for 2 minutes.

Add the wine to the casserole and leave to simmer until the liquid is nearly evaporated, scraping the base of the casserole with a wooden spoon to release all the residue into the sauce.

Pour in the beef stock and return the beef and bacon to the casserole with the tomatoes, carrots, anchovies, orange zest, cinnamon and bouquet garni. Season and cover with the lid or a sheet of foil. Transfer to the oven for 3 hours, or until the meat is super tender and the sauce rich and thickened.

Remove the casserole from the oven, uncover and skim any excess oil from the top. Stir in the olives, then leave to rest and cool overnight.

The next day, mix together the parsley and garlic for the *persillade* with a splash of oil.

To serve, reheat the daube. Divide it among plates with plenty of sauce and spoon over the *persillade* at the last minute.

Cherry and Almond Clafoutis

Clafoutis, though usually associated with cherries, can be made with any seasonal fruit of your choice. In the past I've used apricots, small plums, strawberries and even macerated prunes. You can also experiment with stirring Mediterranean herbs into the batter, such as chopped rosemary, thyme or lemon verbena.

As the base is essentially a batter, once baked the clafoutis needs to be served and eaten swiftly before it deflates and sags. When removed from the oven and then dusted liberally with icing sugar, the sight and aroma is irresistible. I like to roll this out during the summer for a show-stopping end to a barbecue.

Serves 4–6

100g caster sugar, plus 1 tablespoon
  for the cherries
60g ground almonds
20g strong white flour
a pinch of table salt
2 large free-range eggs, plus 3 large
  free-range yolks
275ml double cream
400g ripe cherries, pitted with
  stalks removed
1 tablespoon kirsch
unsalted butter, softened, for
  buttering the dish
icing sugar for dusting
ice cream or whipped cream, to serve

Put the caster sugar, ground almonds, flour and salt in a food processor, and blitz for a minute or so to combine. Add the eggs, extra yolks and cream, then blend to a smooth batter. Pour into a jug and chill for a few hours.

Toss the cherries with the kirsch and the extra caster sugar, and leave to macerate for 10 minutes.

Meanwhile, preheat the oven to 200°C/Fan 180°C/Gas Mark 6. Butter a 22–23cm round ovenproof serving dish or gratin dish. Set aside.

Scatter the cherries over the base of the dish. Stir the batter well, then gently pour evenly over the cherries. Place the dish on a baking sheet, transfer to the oven and bake for 15 minutes, or until risen and golden brown. The middle might not rise as much as the edges, but it should be set.

Dust with icing sugar and serve immediately with something cold and creamy like ice cream or whipped cream.

Focaccia Barese
with olives, tomatoes and anchovies

This sunny focaccia recipe was given to me by a chef friend, Andrea Caputo. His family own a bakery near the beach in Bari on the Puglia coast overlooking the beautiful Adriatic. I've tweaked it slightly with the addition of anchovies and fresh, as opposed to dry, oregano.

The Barese focaccia differs from others in that it has a thinner, slightly crispier dough and uses potatoes in the base to add flavour and texture. It is traditionally baked in a round, pizza style.

Serves 4–6

200g fine semolina flour
100g plain white flour
100g strong white flour, plus
  extra for kneading
10g fresh yeast
300ml lukewarm water
150g floury potatoes, such as King
  Edwards, peeled and cubed
3 tablespoons extra virgin olive oil
olive oil for greasing
sea salt and freshly ground black
  pepper

For the topping
500g cherry vine tomatoes, cut in half
extra virgin olive oil
20 black olives, pitted
100g tin salted anchovies, drained
a handful of fresh oregano leaves

You'll need a 30 x 15cm baking tin, however you can also bake this free-form in a rough round or rectangle on a large baking sheet.

Combine the three flours in the bowl of a stand mixer and set aside. Transfer 100g of this mixture to a separate bowl.

In another small bowl, whisk the yeast in 100ml of the lukewarm water until it dissolves. Pour this over the 100g flour mixture and stir to combine. Wrap the bowl with cling film and leave it to prove in a warm spot for 2 hours, or until starting to bubble on the surface. This is your starter.

Meanwhile, boil the potatoes in salted water until tender, then drain well and roughly mash with a fork. Set aside to cool.

Using the stand mixer, with a kneading hook attached, add the starter to the remaining flour mix. Pour over the remaining water, a little at a time, and beat on low speed to incorporate. Next, add the mashed potatoes and knead until fully combined.

Finally, add the extra virgin olive oil, bit by bit, and then 1 tablespoon salt. The dough will be a bit sticky at this point. Keep kneading in the mixer until the dough is smooth and elastic.

Dust a work surface with flour and transfer the dough onto it. Lightly dust the dough with flour, too, then flatten it slightly and fold it over on itself, letter style. Do this again with the longer sides, then shape the dough into a smooth ball. Place it, seam side down, in a large greased bowl, cover with a tea towel and leave in a warm spot for 3 hours, or until the dough doubles in size.

Grease the baking tin or baking sheet with olive oil. Transfer the risen dough to the tin or baking sheet and use the tips of your greased fingers to spread it out to the edge of the tin or into a circle or rectangle on the baking sheet. Re-cover with the towel and leave it to rise again for 30 minutes.

To make the topping, put the tomatoes in a bowl and season with a splash of extra virgin olive oil and salt and pepper. Use greased fingers to make indentations all over the surface of the dough. Scatter the tomatoes and their juices and the olives over, pressing them in gently. Drizzle with extra virgin olive oil and leave to rise again for 40 minutes.

Meanwhile, preheat the oven to 220°C/Fan 200°C/Gas Mark 7.

Place the focaccia on the middle rack of the oven and bake for 35 minutes, or until puffed up, deeply golden and sounds hollow if you tap the top. Top with the anchovies and transfer to the bottom shelf for 5 minutes to crisp up the edges.

Remove from the oven, sprinkle over the fresh oregano and grind over black pepper, then transfer to a wire rack to cool.

Asparagus, Ricotta and Mint

This is spring on a plate. English asparagus is some of the best in the world, particularly in May and June when naturally in abundance. Here it is cooked very briefly with a little oil and lemon and then served with whipped ricotta and mint to give it a real Mediterranean twist.

I've taken my inspiration from a similar dish I enjoyed in Liguria of fresh broad beans and peas, tossed in grassy olive oil and mint with ricotta, served with hot, charred focaccia straight from the grill.

Serves 4

1 large bunch of asparagus, woody
   ends trimmed off
130g full-fat sheep's or cow's milk
   ricotta (Galbani is a good, readily
   available brand)
leaves from 1 small bunch of mint,
   finely chopped, with some left
   whole, to garnish
grated zest and juice of 1 small
   unwaxed lemon
extra virgin olive oil
toasted ciabatta or focaccia (page 52 or
   shop bought), to serve (optional)
sea salt and freshly ground black
   pepper

Bring a saucepan of salted water to a boil. Plunge in the asparagus and boil for 2 minutes, or until just tender. Remove and drain.

Whisk the ricotta with the chopped mint, lemon zest and half the juice, a splash of extra virgin olive oil and salt and pepper.

To serve, toss the asparagus with some olive oil, the remaining lemon juice and lightly season. Divide among individual plates and add a spoonful of the ricotta, then sprinkle over the remaining mint. Serve as is or with toasted ciabatta or focaccia.

Spaghetti with Datterini Tomatoes
anchovies and sage

This is perhaps the ultimate *spaghetti al pomodoro* – I have made a few little tweaks to add layers of extra flavour. Good ripe tomatoes, such as datterini, are now readily available in supermarkets.

The anchovies add a nice hit of umami. Sage is a happy alternative to basil and works well with the deep-roasted flavours of the tomatoes and chilli. The added dash of syrupy balsamic to the sauce gives sweetness and depth (a good tip for meat ragouts as well).

Further south you'll find this sprinkled with fried day-old breadcrumbs – *pangrattato* – to add a gentle crunch and to soak up any excess sauce into a mushy, crispy deliciousness.

Serves 4

200g seasonal, ripe datterini, cherry
  or other small tomatoes
1 large fresh red chilli, stalk and
  seeds removed
olive oil
3 salted anchovy fillets, rinsed and
  very finely chopped
2 garlic cloves, chopped
leaves from 2 fresh thyme sprigs
200ml tomato passata
½ teaspoon dried chilli flakes,
  or to taste
balsamic vinegar (optional)
400g fresh or dried spaghetti
  or linguine
a handful of sage leaves
30g pecorino or Parmesan cheese,
  finely grated, plus extra to serve
extra virgin olive oil
a handful of day-old breadcrumbs,
  fried in olive oil until golden
  brown (optional, for the southern
  Italian lovers!)
sea salt and freshly ground black
  pepper

Preheat the oven to 200°C/Fan 180°C/ Gas Mark 6.

Place the tomatoes and chilli in a roasting tin, drizzle with olive oil and season well. Sprinkle over the anchovies, garlic and thyme leaves, and roast for 30 minutes, or until the tomatoes are softened.

Transfer everything to a saucepan over a medium heat and pour over the passata. Bring to a boil and then reduce the heat and simmer until the tomatoes start to break up. Season again and sprinkle in chilli flakes to taste. A dash of balsamic here is nice. Keep the sauce hot.

Meanwhile, bring a pan of salted water to the boil. Add the pasta and boil just until al dente. Using tongs, transfer the pasta to the sauce with a couple of ladles of the starchy pasta water. Stir and toss the pasta through to coat, adding the sage, cheese and extra virgin olive oil to taste. Give it another stir. Serve in bowls and sprinkle over more cheese and breadcrumbs, if using.

Sautéed Greens
with herbs, olive oil, lemon and garlic

This is a great way to cook green, leafy vegetables and it's incredibly versatile as you can use whatever greens you have to hand. My combinations might include baby cabbage leaves, spring greens, chard, kale, rocket, celery leaves, even baby gem and cos lettuces. I love to include basil, marjoram or flat-leaf parsley, but choose any herb you love.

Serve this in the summer months, either hot straight from the pan or chilled as an antipasti or side dish. It is particularly good served hot with grilled pork chops.

Serves 4

6 big handfuls of mixed seasonal
   greens, leaves and herbs (see
   introduction, above), rinsed
   if necessary
olive oil
2 garlic cloves, sliced
extra virgin olive oil
juice of 1 lemon
a large pinch of dried chilli
   flakes (optional)
sea salt and freshly ground black
   pepper

Bring a large saucepan of salted water to the boil. Add cabbage leaves, chard and any other similar greens, and boil for 3 minutes, or until just tender. Drain immediately in a colander and refresh under cold running water. This will cool them quickly and retain the colour. Drain well again and squeeze out excess water.

Heat a good splash of olive oil in a large sauté pan or flameproof casserole over a medium heat. When it is hot, add the garlic and stir. As soon as it starts to colour, add the salad leaves followed by the blanched greens.

Cook, moving the greens around the pan with a wooden spoon, for 4–5 minutes. Add the herbs and cook for a further minute.

Remove from the heat and season with salt and pepper and add extra virgin olive oil and lemon juice to taste. Add chilli flakes, if using.

Winter Minestrone
with rosemary

This wonderful winter soup manages to retain its Mediterranean sunshine in style. At once it's both hearty and warming and also vibrant and sun-soaked. I like to eat this on a chilly day with fresh focaccia (page 52) and a blizzard of freshly grated Parmesan on top.

Serves 4–6

olive oil
2 carrots, peeled and roughly chopped
1 celery head, coarsely chopped, with
    the leaves reserved
1 large red onion, coarsely chopped
500g Swiss chard, rinsed,
    stalks roughly chopped and
    leaves shredded
1 garlic bulb, cloves peeled
    and chopped
leaves from a good handful of flat-leaf
    parsley, finely chopped
400g tinned chopped tomatoes
1kg cavolo nero leaves, rinsed
    and shredded
410g tinned cannellini beans,
    drained and rinsed
about 700ml chicken or vegetable
    stock (fresh or homemade is
    best), boiling
needles from 3 fresh rosemary sprigs,
    finely chopped
extra virgin olive oil for drizzling
a handful of finely grated Parmesan
    cheese, to serve
sea salt and freshly ground black
    pepper

Heat a splash of olive oil in a large saucepan over a low heat. When it is hot, add the carrots, celery and onion, and fry until they are softened and caramelised. This will take about 20 minutes, but it's worth the wait for the depth of flavour. Add the chard stalks, garlic and half the parsley leaves, and stir to prevent anything sticking. Stir in the tomatoes, turn up the heat and simmer for 10 minutes, stirring occasionally, or until the liquid is reduced.

Add half the Swiss chard leaves, half the cavolo nero, three-quarters of the cannellini beans and 700ml boiling stock. Bring to the boil, then reduce the heat and simmer for 30 minutes. Pour in more stock, if needed.

Add the remaining Swiss chard leaves, cavolo nero and parsley leaves, and simmer just long enough to blanch briefly so they remain green and crisp. Season to taste.

Transfer the remaining cannellini beans and a ladleful of the cooking liquid to a blender and blitz to make a rough purée. Add this to the soup – it should be very green with a fresh flavour. Stir in the rosemary, drizzle with extra virgin olive oil and sprinkle with Parmesan. Serve.

Grilled Monkfish Tails
with borlotti beans, mussels, focaccia and salsa verde

Both comforting and fresh, this is a slice of perfect Mediterranean cooking – grilled fish on the bone, briny mussels with a chilli hit and a fragrant, punchy salsa verde. The upside-down crowning glory is the day-old grilled bread that sits underneath the fish soaking up all the delicious juices.

Serves 4

olive oil
1 large fresh red chilli, deseeded and finely chopped
1 banana shallot, finely chopped
2 fresh bay leaves
200g fresh mussels, debearded, if necessary, scrubbed and rinsed well in cold water (discard any that do not snap shut when tapped)
50g unsalted butter
a glass of dry white wine
400g tinned borlotti beans, drained and rinsed
4 x 200g monkfish tails on the bone, grey membranes removed
1 lemon, halved
4 pieces of focaccia (page 52 or shop bought), rubbed with olive oil and lightly grilled, to serve
sea salt and freshly ground black pepper

For the salsa verde
½ bunch of chives
½ bunch of mint
½ bunch of flat-leaf parsley, leaves and stalks
120ml extra virgin olive oil
1 tablespoon red wine vinegar
1 teaspoon capers in brine, drained
2 salted anchovy fillets
½ lemon

The salsa verde is best made as soon as possible before serving. Put the chives, mint and parsley in a blender with the olive oil, vinegar, capers and anchovies, and blitz to a rough purée – you want it rustic, not too fine. Squeeze in lemon juice to taste and season with salt and pepper. Set aside at room temperature and do not cover with cling film.

Heat a good splash of olive oil in a saucepan with a tight-fitting lid over a medium-high heat. When it is hot, add the chilli and shallot and stir until softened but without colour. Add the bay leaves followed by the mussels, butter and white wine. Cover and steam the mussels over a medium-high heat until they have just opened (3–5 minutes or so). Remove the mussels from the pan and set aside to cool, discarding any unopened ones. Add the beans to the buttery mussel stock, season well and leave to simmer while you cook the monkfish.

Heat a ridged, cast-iron griddle pan or large sauté pan over a medium heat. Rub the monkfish tails with olive oil and season them with salt and pepper. Add them to the pan and grill for 7–8 minutes to caramelise and cook through, but still be juicy – the flesh will turn opaque and be firm to the touch. Remove the fish from the pan, squeeze over lemon juice to taste and set aside to rest for a couple of minutes.

Pick half of the mussels from the shells and add them to the beans, then squeeze in some lemon juice and check for seasoning. Place the focaccia in serving bowls and top with the beans. Add a monkfish tail and scatter over the mussels still in their shells. Finish with a spoonful of salsa verde.

Chicken Cotoletta (or Milanese)
with roasted datterini tomatoes and gremolata

Here's my take on the classic breaded-and-fried chicken dish, inspired by a delicious version I had in Naples. It was served with slow-roasted sweet tomatoes, extra Parmesan and a punchy gremolata to cut through the richness. This has become a regular menu fixture at some of the Cubitt House pubs and is increasingly tricky to remove due to customer demand. In the winter, when tomatoes are scarce, I like to shred some endive or radicchio lettuce, toss with balsamic and pile on some of the crispy chicken.

This recipe is also a hugely popular option in the Tish household for a special treat – I could eat this every day to be honest but that wouldn't be advisable so I have to save it for special occasions. I think it reminds me of childhood and growing up with Marks and Spencer's crispy chicken goujons or chicken Kievs; it's the ultimate comfort food for me.

You can also use veal or pork. I suggest serving it with fresh pasta or fries (such as my Holiday Chips on page 102) and some aïoli (page 38) to dip on the side.

Serves 4

100g datterini or cherry
    tomatoes, halved
olive oil
150g plain white flour
3 large free-range eggs
170g panko breadcrumbs
40g Parmesan cheese
4 x 150g skinless free-range
    chicken breasts
4 lemon wedges, to serve
a small handful of fresh marjoram or
    oregano leaves, to serve
sea salt and freshly ground black
    pepper

For the gremolata
50ml extra virgin olive oil
1 shallot, finely chopped
2 tablespoons finely chopped flat-leaf
    parsley leaves
1 tablespoon finely chopped fresh
    marjoram or oregano leaves
1 garlic clove, finely chopped
grated zest and juice of ½
    unwaxed lemon

Preheat the oven to 190°C/Fan 170°C/Gas Mark 5.

Lay the tomatoes in a roasting tin, drizzle with olive oil and season. Transfer to the oven and roast for 30–35 minutes until they are softened and caramelised. Reserve.

Meanwhile, tip the flour into one bowl, then crack and beat the eggs in a second bowl. Add the breadcrumbs to a third bowl and finely grate in half of the Parmesan, then stir to combine.

To make the gremolata, simply mix everything together and reserve.

When you are ready to cook, place the chicken breasts on a board and cover with a double layer of cling film. Bash with a saucepan to flatten them to 0.5cm thick, then season with salt. Coat the flattened breasts in the flour, then the egg and finally in the cheesy breadcrumb mixture, patting it on until they are thoroughly coated.

Heat a thin layer of olive oil in a large frying pan over a medium heat. When it is hot, add the chicken pieces and fry for 3–4 minutes on each side until the meat is cooked through and they are golden. Do this in batches, if necessary, and keep warm in the turned-off oven.

Transfer the chicken breasts to kitchen paper to drain, then season with sea salt.

Serve with the tomatoes and gremolata spooned over, lemon wedges for squeezing over and the remaining Parmesan for grating over, if you wish. Lastly add a sprinkle of marjoram or oregano leaves.

Tuscan-style Steak
with rosemary, garlic and grape molasses

A culinary hymn of praise to simplicity, this is my favourite way to cook steak. Fiorentina is traditionally a T-bone or a porterhouse steak – a steak on the bone has more flavour than a boneless one – but a good-quality rib-eye or sirloin steak will work well. The steak must be cut thick as you want the meat beautifully crisp and caramelised on the outside and medium-rare and pink within. This recipe is perfect for cooking on the barbecue, and fried potatoes and a salad are ideal accompaniments. Try my Holiday Chips (page 102) with this for a real treat.

Serves 4

2 x 1kg T-bone or porterhouse steaks,
   or 2 x 600g sirloin or rump steaks,
   at room temperature
olive oil
4 garlic cloves, finely chopped
needles from 3 fresh rosemary sprigs,
   finely chopped
grated zest and juice of 1
   unwaxed lemon
2 tablespoons grape or date
   molasses (optional)
sea salt and freshly ground black
   pepper

Light a barbecue about 30 minutes before you want to cook so the coals turn ashen grey and are at the optimum grilling temperature. Position the grill above the coals so it gets very hot. Alternatively, heat a large ridged, cast-iron griddle pan to maximum.

Rub the steaks with oil, then season well and place them on the grill or griddle pan. Cook for 3 minutes on each side, or until nicely caramelised and charred. Now move either the steaks to a cooler spot on the barbecue or turn the heat under the griddle down to medium, and continue cooking for a further 6–7 minutes, turning every minute or so for medium-rare. Add another 3–4 minutes for medium-well.

Remove the steaks from the grill and transfer to a tray or rimmed platter and sprinkle over the garlic, rosemary, lemon zest and juice and the molasses, if using. Leave to rest for 10 minutes like this before serving either whole or in the traditional style with the meat cut from the bone, sliced and arranged back against the bone for serving with the resting juices spooned over. Sprinkle with extra salt, if you want.

Maritozzi

Maritozzi are the infamous overstuffed cream buns hailing from Rome. The original dates back to medieval days in Rome where a dairy-free version filled with dried fruit and nuts was eaten during Lent. The lightly sweetened, cream-laden bun was said to have been used to hide a ring during a marriage proposal.

If you've been to Rome, or most anywhere in Lazio, you'll have seen them lined up on counters at neighbourhood cafés and bakeries: large, shiny, golden-brown brioche-style buns brimming with whipped cream or *crème pâtissérie* smeared over the slit in the surface. Add any fruit or jam you like to the filling.

Serves 12

For the leaven
7g sachet fast-action dried yeast
60g strong white flour
150ml whole milk, lukewarm
1 tablespoon clear honey

For the dough
400g strong white flour, plus extra
    for dusting
100g plain white flour
100g caster sugar
2 teaspoons table salt
2 large free-range eggs, plus
    1 large free-range yolk
100ml lukewarm water
70ml light olive oil, plus extra for
    the bowl
grated zest of 1 unwaxed orange
2 tablespoons clear honey, to glaze

To finish
300ml double cream
3 tablespoons icing sugar, plus extra
    for sprinkling
grated zest of 1 unwaxed orange
1 teaspoon ground cinnamon

First make the leaven. Mix the yeast and flour together in a bowl, then add the milk and honey and whisk until you have a smooth mixture. Cover the bowl with cling film and set aside for 30 minutes. You will see bubbles forming.

To make the dough, put both flours in a large bowl and stir in the caster sugar and salt. Combine 1 of the eggs, extra yolk, water, olive oil and orange zest in a separate bowl, and whisk to mix together.

Once the leaven is bubbling, add it to the oil and egg mix, then pour the liquids into the flour and use your hands to bring everything together and form a soft dough. Place the dough on a lightly oiled surface – alternatively, you can do this process in a stand mixer. Knead for a few minutes until you have a smooth but sticky dough.

Wash, dry and grease the bowl with olive oil. Roll the dough into a ball and place in the bowl. Cover with cling film and leave to rise in a warm place for up to 2 hours, or until doubled in size.

Line a baking sheet with baking parchment and set aside.

Knock back and scrape the dough out of the bowl onto a lightly floured surface. Roll it into a thick log, then use a dough cutter or knife to divide it into 12 equal pieces, each one about 80g. Shape each piece into a ball (cup the dough on the work surface and roll in your hand lightly) and then place on the baking sheet, a few centimetres apart. Cover with greased cling film (to make sure the cling film doesn't stick to the buns). Leave the buns to rise for an hour, or until doubled in size.

Meanwhile, preheat the oven to 200°C /Fan 180°C /Gas Mark 6, and gently beat the remaining egg in a small bowl.

Remove the cling film from the baking sheet and brush the buns with the beaten egg. Transfer to the oven and bake for 15 minutes, or until they are golden brown and risen. Transfer the buns to a wire rack and brush them with the honey while still warm.

Whip the cream to soft peaks and fold in the icing sugar and orange zest.

Leave the buns to cool slightly before cutting a deep slit down the middle, and filling with whipped cream. I like to get a classic smooth finish that makes them appear huge and impressively overstuffed. A palette knife dipped in hot water to smooth the cream and a little patience is all that's required. Finish with extra icing sugar and ground cinnamon sprinkled over.

My Tiramisu

Originally from Trentino, the tiramisu is now an Italian classic and popular around the world. Interestingly for a chef and cookery writer who focuses on the food of the Mediterranean, I've never published a tiramisu recipe before, which is strange as I've been making them for years and in all shapes and forms.

This is the recipe I used to make at Al Duca restaurant a few years back – simple and utterly indulgent. A proper tiramisu is made with the best mascarpone and very good coffee. It's important to let the tiramisu sit in the fridge for a good few hours to set and for the flavours to develop. Serve with a glass of marsala.

Serves 4–6

3 large free-range egg yolks
100g caster sugar
500g full-fat mascarpone
200ml extra strong black coffee
   (freshly brewed, not instant!)
100ml sweet marsala
25ml dark rum
26 Savoiardi biscuits or ladyfingers
dark cocoa powder for dusting
20g 70% dark chocolate for finely
   grating over

Whisk together the egg yolks and caster sugar in a stand mixer until pale and fluffy, or use a hand whisk. Fold in the mascarpone until fully incorporated. Reserve.

Pour the coffee into a wide bowl, adding the marsala and rum.

Choose your serving container – either a large dish for everyone to share from, or use individual bowls.

Dip half the biscuits into the coffee, soaking the biscuits through but not so much that they turn mushy – a few seconds only.

Layer the biscuits in the dish to cover the base, then top with half the mascarpone mix, spreading evenly over the top. Repeat with the remaining biscuits and finally finish with the second layer of mascarpone. Spread it evenly over, then dust with cocoa powder.

Cover the bowl with cling film and chill for at least 6 hours, but ideally overnight. This process really helps the flavours to develop and the consistency to be perfect.

Serve straight from the fridge with a final dusting of cocoa powder and a grating of dark chocolate.

Carinola Bread

This is the traditional flatbread of Slovenia – a simple, delicious white bread flavoured with caraway, honey and extra virgin olive oil. It's a bread to be torn at the table and shared, dipped in olive oil or used to mop up juicy remains from stews. I highly recommend this with the pork belly *jota* (page 79).

Makes 1 loaf

2 x 7g sachets fast-action dried yeast
4 teaspoons clear honey
350ml milk, lukewarm
600g strong white flour
2 teaspoons table salt
1 tablespoon extra virgin olive oil,
   plus extra for the bowl
1 large free-range egg, beaten
1 teaspoon caraway seeds
sea salt

Stir the yeast and honey into the lukewarm milk, until dissolved, then leave for an hour, or until it becomes frothy and bubbly.

Put the flour and salt into the bowl of a stand mixer with a dough hook attached, or a large bowl, and make a well in the centre. Add the yeast mixture and olive oil to the well and beat on low speed or use your hands to knead until a smooth, elastic dough forms. Shape the dough into a rough ball and set aside.

Wash and dry the bowl, then grease the inside with olive oil. Return the dough to the bowl, cover with a tea towel and set aside in a warm place for an hour, or until it doubles in size.

Knock back the dough and turn it out onto a lightly floured surface, then transfer it onto a baking sheet. Use your hands to press the dough into a rough round, then stretch until you have a 1.5cm thick circle. Brush with the egg and sprinkle with the caraway seeds and sea salt. Cover with a tea towel and leave for 25 minutes or so to lightly prove.

Meanwhile, preheat the oven to 220°C/Fan 200°C/Gas Mark 7.

Transfer the baking sheet to the oven and bake the bread for 25 minutes, or until it is beautifully golden brown and sounds hollow when tapped on the bottom. Leave to cool completely on a wire rack before serving.

Potato, Onion and Sheep's Cheese Torte
with thyme, rosemary and slow-cooked garlic

Frika is a Slovenian staple across the country. It's a rösti-esque assembly with a stuffing or topping – inland cooks tend to use pork fat in the potatoes, but this coastal version uses olive oil as its base with chopped spring onions and Mediterranean herbs. I've also had this stuffed with prawns, mussels and fresh chilli. This makes an indulgent breakfast with a crispy, golden-yolk fried egg.

Serves 4

6 large garlic cloves
olive oil
400g Desiree potatoes
1 bunch small spring onions, sliced
    thinly, including the green ends
a handful of fresh rosemary needles,
    finely chopped
leaves from 6 fresh thyme
    sprigs, chopped
grated zest of ½ unwaxed lemon
250g semi-hard pecorino, such as
    Romano, or other sheep's cheese,
    finely grated
50g Parmesan cheese, finely grated
10 sage leaves, roughly chopped
4 eggs, fried, to serve (optional)
sea salt and freshly ground black
    pepper

Preheat the oven to 180°C/Fan 160°C/Gas Mark 4.

Place the garlic cloves in a small oven tray, drizzle with oil and bake for 40 minutes, or until the cloves are soft and tender. Set them aside to cool, then squeeze the roasted garlic flesh from the skins, chop and set aside.

Turn up the oven temperature to 200°C/Fan 180°C/Gas Mark 6.

Meanwhile, peel the potatoes and grate them directly onto a tea towel. Gather up the towel and twist and squeeze to extract all the moisture from the potatoes. Transfer them to a bowl and season well with salt and pepper. Stir in 4 tablespoons of olive oil, the spring onions, half the rosemary needles and thyme leaves and the lemon zest.

Heat a good splash of olive oil in an ovenproof sauté pan over a medium heat. When it is hot, add half the potato mixture, pressing into the pan to compact. Cook for 8 minutes to slowly soften the potatoes and lightly brown the base – you can peek underneath to check. Sprinkle over the cheeses and roasted garlic and continue cooking for a further 3–4 minutes to fully brown and set the base.

Sprinkle over the remaining potato mixture, press this down on top of the cheese to compact again. Transfer the pan to the oven for 8 minutes, then sprinkle over the remaining rosemary and thyme and arrange the sage leaves on top. Put the pan back in the oven for 2 minutes to finish cooking – you want the top beautifully golden brown and the potatoes completely cooked.

Remove from the oven and leave the *frika* to cool a little, then carefully slide it onto a serving plate and cut into portions. Serve with extra sea salt for sprinkling over, with a fried egg on the side, if you like.

Baked Butter Beans
with tomatoes, eggs, smoked paprika and tender greens

This dish falls somewhere between traditional baked beans and shakshuka (eggs baked with a piquant red pepper stew). Tender greens and herbs add a fresh vibrancy, while the hot smoky kick of paprika and the mellow sweet honey add a lovely backdrop to the rich oozing eggs. It's a breakfast favourite in my house.

You will also find this served with chopped smoked pork or *lardo* (Italian cured fatback), which has been fried and is then added into the sauce at the start of the process along with the onions and garlic. I think a hearty bread, such as Carinola (page 70), is ideal to serve with this.

Serves 4

olive oil
2 garlic cloves, crushed
1 red onion, thinly sliced
200g chard, spinach or spring greens,
   washed, trimmed and
   finely chopped
400g tinned butter beans, drained
   and rinsed
400g tinned chopped tomatoes
1 small fresh red chilli, deseeded
   and finely chopped
1 tablespoon clear honey
1 teaspoon ground cinnamon
2 teaspoons hot smoked paprika
4 large free-range eggs
sea salt and freshly ground black
   pepper

To serve
a handful of fresh dill fronds,
   roughly chopped
a handful of fresh flat-leaf parsley
   leaves, finely chopped
extra virgin olive oil

Preheat the oven to 200°C/Fan 180°C/Gas Mark 6.

Heat a splash of olive oil in a large ovenproof sauté pan or flameproof casserole over a medium heat. When it is hot, add the garlic and onion with plenty of salt and pepper and fry, stirring for 2–3 minutes until the onion is softened but not coloured. Toss in the greens and stir for a further 3–4 minutes.

Add the beans, tomatoes, chilli, honey, cinnamon and smoked paprika. Season again and stir to combine. If you think it's a little dry, add half a cup of water and stir in – the mixture should have a saucy consistency.

Bring to a simmer, then carefully crack in the 4 eggs, putting them an even distance apart so they each essentially have a quarter of the pan. Transfer the pan to the oven and bake for 20 minutes, or until the edges brown and the flavours intensify. The eggs should be just set, because you still want the yolks runny.

Remove the pan from the oven, scatter over the dill and parsley and drizzle with extra virgin olive oil for good measure.

Steamed Clams
with parsley and garlic

Clams are my favourite shellfish, and the clear Istrian coastal waters are abundant with clams and other shellfish. I find the sweet, slightly chewy meat delectable. The sauce for this is very familiar – white wine, lots of garlic and fresh parsley, but with the addition of chilli flakes and fried breadcrumbs. The breadcrumbs not only add texture, but also soak up the sweet, briny, herb-flecked juices, ensuring nothing goes to waste. If you can't get clams, mussels work equally as well.

Serves 4 as a starter

500g live palourde clams or
    mussels, scrubbed, bearded, if
    necessary, and rinsed well in cold
    running water
olive oil
a good handful of dried white
    breadcrumbs
2 garlic cloves, finely chopped
a glass of dry white wine
¼ teaspoon dried chilli flakes
75ml extra virgin olive oil
2 large handfuls of flat-leaf parsley,
    leaves and stalks roughly chopped,
    to finish
freshly grated black pepper

Discard any open clams or mussels that do not shut when sharply tapped.

Heat a good splash of olive oil in a sauté pan over a medium heat. When it is hot, add the breadcrumbs and fry, stirring, until golden brown. Tip them onto kitchen paper to drain and set aside.

Heat a large saucepan over a high heat. Throw in the clams with the garlic, white wine and chilli flakes. Place the lid on top and steam for 5 minutes, shaking the pan as you go.

Uncover the pan and remove any unopened clams or mussels – give them a tap and if they still don't open, discard them. Pour in the extra virgin olive oil, grind in some black pepper and stir through with the clams and the juices.

Stir in the parsley, then transfer the clams to serving bowls and pour over all the cooking liquid. Spoon over the fried breadcrumbs and serve.

Istrian-style Gnocchi
with bottarga, bay leaves and dried chillies

Traganci, a traditional Baltic dumpling not dissimilar to gnocchi, takes its culinary bedfellows from its location. Move inland and you are likely to find this laden with fried pork, mountain herbs and a rich cheese sauce. But on the Adriatic coast it takes on a much more familiar Mediterranean feel with extra virgin olive oil, aromatic bay and sage, chilli flakes and the sweet, salty kick of bottarga – the dried salted fish roe, more commonly associated with southern Italian cooking, but well used in Slovenian coastal cuisine.

The dumplings are incredibly versatile. I add them into slow-cooked meat dishes or serve them in a sauce, as I would serve gnocchi or pasta.

Serves 4

500g 00 flour, plus extra for dusting
150g fine semolina flour
3 large free-range eggs, beaten
100ml extra virgin olive oil
75–85ml whole milk
olive oil for greasing a tray
5 fresh bay leaves
½ lemon
a handful of flat-leaf parsley leaves
25g bottarga, finely grated
1 heaped teaspoon dried chilli flakes
sea salt and freshly ground black
    pepper

Mix the 00 flour and semolina flour together in a bowl with a good amount of salt and pepper. Make a well in the centre and stir in the eggs, pulling in the flour. Now slowly pour in 50ml of the olive oil and mix in enough milk to make a soft dough. Cover the bowl and leave the dough to relax for 20 minutes.

Meanwhile, bring a saucepan of salted water to the boil. Lightly grease a baking tray with olive oil, and set aside. Preheat the oven to a low setting to keep the *traganci* hot as they are cooked.

Using a greased dessertspoon, scoop up some dough and drop it into the boiling water. Continue until you have as many *traganci* in the pan as it will hold without overcrowding. The dough will sink and then rise to the surface when they are cooked. Use a slotted spoon to transfer the *traganci* to the greased tray and keep warm in the oven. Repeat the process until you've used all the dough, bringing the water back to the boil between batches.

Heat the remaining 50ml olive oil in a large sauté pan over a medium heat. When it is hot, add the *traganci* and bay leaves and season with salt and pepper. Cook for 2–3 minutes, turning here and there as you go, until they are all lightly coloured. Now squeeze in lemon juice, add a splash of water and cook for a further minute or so.

Stir in the parsley and then turn off the heat. Sprinkle over the bottarga and chilli flakes, then transfer to bowls for serving.

Slow-roasted Pork Belly
with white beans, sweet pickled turnips, potatoes and bay leaves

A robust and tasty slow-cooked dish ideal for the colder months. It's also a one-pot job, which I love, and is incredibly therapeutic to make in the winter months. There's something about building and capturing different layers of flavour all in one place, with the result being more than a sum of the parts. I place a steaming pot of this on the table along with some Carinola Bread (page 70) to mop up the juices. The sweet pickled turnips add a distinctive sweet-sour flavour to the dish, and you can buy them in Middle Eastern supermarkets and online.

Serves 4

olive oil
500g pork belly, skin on, cut into
    4 equal pieces
4 dried bay leaves
4 cloves
3 garlic cloves, crushed and chopped
1 onion, finely chopped
150g new potatoes, scrubbed and
    coarsely chopped
2 teaspoons sweet smoked paprika
a glass of dry white wine
4 dried thyme sprigs
1 tablespoon clear honey
800ml chicken stock (fresh or
    homemade is best)
400g tinned white beans, drained
    and rinsed
120g sweet pickled turnips from
    a jar, drained
a large handful of seasonal greens,
    such as chard, curly kale or
    spinach, washed, trimmed and
    roughly chopped
sea salt and freshly ground black
    pepper

Preheat the oven to 170°C/Fan 150°C/Gas Mark 3.

Heat a splash of oil in a large flameproof casserole over a medium heat. When it is hot, add the pork belly pieces, skin side down, and sear for 4–5 minutes until nicely browned before turning over and colouring on the underside. Transfer the pork to a plate and set aside.

Add the bay leaves, cloves, garlic and onion to the porky oil, and stir for a few minutes until the onion is softened but without colour. Now stir in the potatoes and paprika and keep stirring for a minute or two to cook out the paprika.

Return the pork to the casserole with any juices, along with the wine, thyme sprigs and honey. Bring to the boil and reduce the wine and cooking juices until they are almost evaporated. Add the stock and return to the boil, then reduce the heat to a simmer. Cover the casserole and transfer it to the oven for 1½ hours. After this time, check the pork – it should be soft and tender, and the stock reduced by about half. If it's not quite there, pop it back in the oven for another 20 minutes or so and check again.

Place the casserole on the hob over a medium heat. Stir in the white beans and pickled turnips, and season well with salt and pepper. Simmer for 7 minutes or so to blend all the flavours together. Stir in the greens and simmer about 2 minutes longer. Turn off the heat, re-cover and leave to stand for 10 minutes or so until the greens are tender. Check the seasoning, and serve.

Pear and Poppy Seed Torte

Koper is a beautiful seaside town on the Slovenian coast. It boasts fantastic cafés and restaurants selling traditional and Mediterranean-influenced Slovenian dishes. Pekarna Europa bakery makes these tortes twice daily, usually with apples, but occasionally quinces. On one of my visits, I was served one with cultured cream. It was warm, moist and delicious. The bakers had used a distinctive local and potent pear *eau de vie* for flavouring, but brandy will do just fine.

Poppy seeds feature heavily in traditional Slovenian cookery, both sweet and savoury, and work particularly well with pears and apples.

Makes 6–8 slices

2 large free-range egg yolks, beaten
80g caster sugar
50g unsalted butter, 30g melted
   and 20g chopped, plus extra for
   buttering the cake tin
150ml whole milk
125ml dry white wine
1 teaspoon vanilla extract
grated zest of 1 unwaxed lemon
200g plain white flour
2 teaspoons baking powder
6 small, sweet pears, such as Comice
   or William
2 tablespoons fruit jam, such as
   pear or apricot
1 tablespoon pear *eau de vie* or brandy
2 teaspoons poppy seeds
sea salt
icing sugar for dusting

Whisk the eggs, sugar and the 30g melted butter together in a bowl. Add milk, wine, vanilla and lemon zest, and whisk together. Sift over the flour and baking powder with a pinch of salt and continue whisking so there are no lumps – you'll have a thin batter. Leave to rest for 20 minutes.

Meanwhile, preheat the oven to 180°C/Fan 160°C/Gas Mark 4. Grease the base and sides of a 21cm springform cake tin, around 10cm deep.

Peel, quarter and core the pears. Cut each quarter into segments. Gently heat the jam in a small saucepan and stir in the *eau de vie*.

Pour half the batter into the cake tin. Arrange half the pear slices on top, dot with 10g of the chopped butter and sprinkle over half the poppy seeds. Pour over the jam and *eau de vie* mixture, then add the remaining batter. Arrange the remaining pear slices on top and dot with the remaining 10g of chopped butter and sprinkle over the remaining poppy seeds.

Transfer to the oven and bake for 1 hour, or until the cake is just firm to the touch with a little wobble in the centre. Remove from the oven and leave to cool in the tin on a wire rack for 30 minutes before removing from the tin. Sift over icing sugar after it's completely cool, then serve.

Potica

honey, walnut, goat's curd and chocolate bread

Here's a real showstopper of a recipe. Traditionally made at Christmastime, this historic sweet bread has plenty of good things in it. There are many versions, but the staple ingredients are the sweet dough and the walnuts. You can replace the walnuts with a mix of pistachios and hazelnuts, and you can also throw in some chopped sour cherries, dates or candied citrus zest. I think this is delicious with anything creamy.

The kugelhof tin isn't essential – and is certainly not traditional – but it does create a beautiful and rather majestic effect.

Makes 8–10 slices

185ml whole milk, lukewarm
190g dark demerara sugar, plus
   1 teaspoon
7g sachet fast-action dried yeast
400g plain white flour, plus extra
   for rolling out
½ teaspoon table salt
170g unsalted butter, chopped, plus
   extra for buttering the tin
3 large free-range egg yolks, beaten,
   plus 1 large free-range egg white,
   lightly whisked
5 tablespoons dark rum
250g shelled walnut halves
3 tablespoons clear honey
2 teaspoons ground cinnamon
125ml whole milk, chilled
60g goat's curd
40g 70% dark chocolate, grated
icing sugar, to decorate (optional)

Mix 60ml of the lukewarm milk, 1 teaspoon demerara sugar and the yeast together in a bowl. Set aside for 10 minutes, or until frothy and bubbling.

In the bowl of a stand mixer, with the dough hook attached, or in a separate large bowl, combine the flour, 120g of the demerara sugar and the salt. Rub in 120g of the butter until it resembles fine breadcrumbs. Pour in the yeast mixture, egg yolks, 1 tablespoon of the rum and the remaining lukewarm milk. Knead on low speed or with your hands for 8–10 minutes until the dough is smooth. Cover the bowl with a tea towel and set aside in a warm place to prove for 2 hours, or until it doubles in size.

Meanwhile, generously butter the inside of a 22cm kugelhopf or Bundt tin or a 22cm springform cake tin 10cm deep. Set aside.

Put the walnuts in a food processor and blitz until finely chopped, then add the remaining 70g demerara sugar, honey, cinnamon, the remaining rum and the remaining butter, and process until fully combined. Bring the chilled milk to a simmer in a saucepan over medium heat. Add the walnut mixture and stir for 10 minutes, or until nice and thick. Pour the mixture into a bowl and set aside to cool.

When the walnut mixture is cool, stir in the goat's curd, chocolate and whisked egg white.

Turn the dough out onto a lightly floured work surface and use a floured rolling pin to roll into a 48 x 33cm rectangle. Spread over the walnut mixture, leaving a 0.5cm border on the edges. Starting from one long side, roll up to enclose the filling. Very gently coil the rolled dough into the kugelhopf, Bundt or springform tin, seam-side in or down so it will seal while baking.

Cover with a tea towel and set aside to prove for 1 hour, or until the dough reaches to the top of the tin.

Meanwhile, preheat the oven to 200°C/Fan 180°C/Gas Mark 6.

Place in the oven and bake for 35–40 minutes until the cake sounds hollow when tapped. Leave to cool in the tin for 5 minutes, then turn out and transfer to a wire rack until completely cool. Sift over icing sugar, if you like, then slice and serve.

Burek

with honey-roasted pumpkin, goat's cheese and mint

The *burek* is a popular dish found throughout the Middle East, the Istrian Balkans and North Africa, taking many shapes and forms. The pastry is always filo or *warqa*, whether baked into a pie like I've done here, snaked like a coil or made into individual pastries. It can be meat, vegetable, sweet or savoury. Mine, which sits in both the sweet and savoury camps, uses sweet, honey-roasted pumpkin that is offset with salty cheese, some punchy North African pepper and green pistachios for a spike of emerald. Buy a heavy, fleshed variety of pumpkin that will be sweeter and give more flavour. I like to serve this warm with nothing more than a little fresh salad of cucumber and dill and perhaps some yoghurt.

Serves 12

olive oil
800g pumpkin, such as Delicia or
    iron bark, peeled, deseeded and cut
    into bite-sized chunks
2 tablespoons clear honey
a pinch of Aleppo pepper flakes
leaves from ½ small bunch of mint,
    finely chopped
300g soft chèvre-style goat's cheese
12 sheets filo pastry
100ml whole milk
1 large free-range egg
a handful of shelled green pistachio
    nuts, roughly chopped
sea salt and freshly ground black
    pepper

Preheat the oven to 210°C/Fan 190°C/Gas Mark 7. Grease a baking tin with olive oil – I use a nonstick 30cm springform tin 7.5cm deep.

Put the pumpkin into a roasting tin, drizzle with honey, some olive oil and season with salt and black pepper, then sprinkle over the Aleppo pepper flakes. Roast the pumpkin for 25 minutes, or until it is tender and caramelised. Transfer it to a mixing bowl and mix in the mint leaves and goat's cheese. Season to taste, add a splash of olive oil and mix. Set aside.

Do not turn the oven off.

Layer half the filo pastry sheets on top of each other in the greased tin – ensure some of the pastry hangs over the edge. Brush each layer with a little milk. Turn the tray slightly for each layer, so there is a full pastry overhang around the whole tin.

Next, add the pumpkin filling. Layer the remaining sheets of filo pastry over the top using the same method of arranging overhanging pastry and brushing with milk.

When all the pastry has been used, roll over the pastry edges to seal the edges. Beat the egg with the remaining milk, then brush this mixture over the top and rolled pastry edge. Sprinkle with the pistachios.

Place on a baking sheet and transfer to the oven. Bake for 35 minutes, or until piping hot, beautifully crisp and golden brown. Leave to cool on a wire rack for at least 30 minutes before removing from the tin. Serve warm or at room temperature, cut into slices.

Braised Peas and Fennel
with savoury

My natural way to cook peas is to simmer briefly just to take the bite out of them. This recipe, however, calls for a slow braise with wine, fennel and stock until the peas become very soft and tender, almost collapsing into the delicious juices. Discovering and then developing this dish highlighted two things for me – slow cooking peas like this is a very good thing indeed, and peas and fennel have a natural affinity when cooked together, giving a lovely blend of sweet, fragrant and aromatic.

I finish this dish with summer savoury, a wonderful Mediterranean herb, part of the mint family (an integral ingredient in the *herbes de Provence* mix) that has a sweet-hot, peppery kick. If you struggle to find summer savoury, replace it with a mixture of sage and thyme.

Serves 6–8 as a side dish
or 4–6 as a main course

olive oil
1 small onion, finely sliced
1 large or 2 small fennel bulbs,
    quartered lengthways and then
    each quarter cut into 4 strips
70ml dry white wine
70ml vegetable stock (fresh or
    homemade is best)
400g shelled fresh or frozen peas
grated zest of ½ unwaxed lemon
a handful of summer savoury leaves,
    or 8 sage leaves and 1 teaspoon fresh
    thyme leaves
sea salt and freshly ground black
    pepper

Heat a flameproof casserole over a medium heat with enough olive oil to cover the base by about 0.5cm. When it is hot, add the onion and fry for 4–5 minutes, stirring as you go, until it is softened but without colour. Now add the fennel, season lightly with salt and pepper and stir for a further 3–4 minutes. Add the wine and boil until it reduces by half, then pour in the stock and simmer for 10–12 minutes until the fennel is nice and tender.

Add the peas and leave to simmer for 10 minutes. The liquid should be nearly evaporated – if it's still too liquid, then boil for a further 2–3 minutes.

Stir in the lemon zest, summer savoury and adjust the seasoning, then serve.

Mussels Marinated in White Wine and Vinegar
with chilli flakes and thyme

Many Mediterranean coastal towns have age-old recipes for pickling and preserving seafoods – a necessity in days before refrigeration. These marinated mussels are a Croatian version of the Spanish *escabeche*, in which seafood is lightly cooked and then plunged into a sweet-sharp bath of vinegar, wine, spices and oil. The mussels act like a sponge, soaking up all the flavours. These make an excellent snack served with pre-dinner drinks or as part of an antipasti.

In tavernas along the coastal towns of Croatia you'll see plates and plates of these mussels surrounded by empty black shells, deliberately presented to be used as pincers to pick up these little delicacies.

Serves 4

1kg live mussels, debearded, if
    necessary, scrubbed and rinsed
    well in cold water
100ml dry white wine
200ml light extra virgin olive oil
6 fresh thyme sprigs
2 fresh bay leaves
1 cinnamon stick
1 fresh rosemary sprig
1 teaspoon black peppercorns
½ garlic head, separated into
    unpeeled cloves
peeled zest of ½ unwaxed lemon, cut
    into thin strips
100ml white wine vinegar, such
    as muscatel
½ teaspoon dried chilli flakes
½ tablespoon sea salt

Discard any open mussels that do not snap shut when sharply tapped. Put all the remaining mussels and white wine in a large saucepan with a tight-fitting lid over a medium-high heat. Cover the pan and leave the mussels to steam for 6–7 minutes until they have all opened.

Tip the mussels into a sieve set over a large bowl and leave until cool enough to handle, then remove them from the shells and transfer to a heatproof bowl. Discard any mussels that have not opened. (Use a fine sieve to strain the reserved mussel cooking liquid if you want it for another use, such as using in a stock or sauce.) If you want to use the shells for serving, give them a good wash and set aside.

Meanwhile, combine the extra virgin olive oil, thyme, bay leaves, cinnamon stick, rosemary, black peppercorns, garlic and lemon zest in a saucepan over a medium-low heat, and leave for about 8 minutes until gently bubbling.

Remove the pan from the heat and add the vinegar, chilli flakes and salt.

While the marinade is still hot, pour it over the shucked mussels and stir to combine. Leave to cool, then cover the bowl with cling film and let the mussels marinate in the fridge for 24 hours before serving.

Barbecued Scallops
with brown butter

Scallops are a real delicacy in Croatia. The fresh salty water of the Adriatic produces shellfish that are world-class, celebrated in the riotously joyous annual Kapesante of Novigrad scallop festival.

This recipe is inspired by ones I enjoyed at that festival; the scallops were cooked in a shell over a fire. The shells are brilliant vessels to serve the scallops in – they conduct the heat gently, protecting the delicate flesh – and they look great, too. Cooking them over a barbecue produces a little waft of gentle smoke, which I love, but you can also cook these successfully in a searing-hot griddle pan on the hob.

Serves 4 as a starter

12 hand-dived scallops with roe, on the half shell, or shucked from a whole shell and placed on a half shell – a fishmonger can do this for you
180g unsalted butter, cut into 12 pieces
20g panko breadcrumbs
½ lemon
leaves from ½ bunch of flat-leaf parsley, very finely chopped
bread, to serve
sea salt and freshly ground black pepper

Light a barbecue about 30 minutes before you want to cook so the coals turn ashen grey and are at the optimum grilling temperature. Position the grill above the coals so it gets very hot. Alternatively, heat a large ridged, cast-iron griddle pan to maximum.

Season the scallops with salt and pepper and place a piece of butter to the side of each scallop. Sprinkle over the breadcrumbs and transfer the scallops to the grill.

Cook for about 5 minutes, then spoon over some of the butter. When the butter starts to foam and turn a nut-brown colour, squeeze over the lemon juice – this seasons the scallops and stops the butter burning – and sprinkle over the parsley. When the scallops are just cooked (they'll give a little spring back when pressed with a finger), the shells are browned and the butter is foaming, use tongs to remove them from the grill and serve straightaway. Be careful not to spill any of the melted butter. Some good bread is ideal for mopping up the buttery juices.

Pot-roasted Pork Shoulder and Potatoes
with bitter leaves and hazelnuts

This pork dish epitomises the big, hearty, flavoured rustic cooking of Croatia. Pork shoulder requires long, slow cooking to yield its delicious, succulent meat.

Here it is pot-roasted with wine, vinegar and herbs to create its own delicious gravy. Potatoes, kale and crunchy hazelnuts are added towards the end of the cooking to create a flavourful one-pot dish. I love how the herby, vinegary, porky aromas waft through the kitchen, giving out warm hugs to all who pass by.

If your pork shoulder is too big to fit in the pan, then feel free to halve it as necessary and then reduce the cooking time by 40 minutes or so.

Serves 4–6

olive oil
1 boneless pork shoulder with a
    good layer of fat, 1–1.2kg, halved if
    necessary, see introduction above
4 fresh bay leaves
4 garlic cloves, crushed
4 fresh rosemary sprigs
500ml dry red wine
150ml red wine vinegar, such as
    cabernet sauvignon
450g Desiree potatoes, scrubbed and
    thickly sliced
100g curly kale or cavolo nero, rinsed
    and roughly chopped
60g toasted shelled hazelnuts,
    roughly chopped
a handful of sage leaves, chopped
sea salt and freshly ground black
    pepper

Preheat the oven to 160°C/Fan 140°C/Gas Mark 3.

Heat a good splash of olive oil in a flameproof casserole over a medium heat. When it is hot, add the pork, fat side down, and brown for 6–7 minutes. Turn it over and repeat on the underside. Now add the bay leaves, garlic cloves and rosemary, and stir for a minute or two before adding the wine and vinegar.

Bring the liquid to a boil, scraping the bottom of the pan as you go to release any sediment, and continue boiling until it reduces by half.

Cover the casserole and transfer it to the oven for 80 minutes. At this point, check the meat with the tip of a sharp knife – it should be starting to become tender. Place the potatoes around the pork, put the lid back on and return the casserole to the oven for a further 35 minutes.

Remove the casserole from the oven and uncover – the pork should be meltingly tender and the potatoes cooked with a rich, tasty gravy. Add the greens, hazelnuts and sage, and season well with salt and pepper. Re-cover and leave for 10 minutes to rest before serving, family style. The greens will cook in the residual heat.

Winter Pasta
with beef cheeks, red wine and a wild mushroom ragout

A beautifully robust pasta dish from the Dubrovnik area of Croatia. I use beef cheeks as I find the texture and flavour unbeatable, but you can also use chuck or a braising steak to great effect. A selection of cultivated 'wild' mushrooms give a lovely earthy flavour and a pleasing variety of textures to this rustic dish. Chestnut mushrooms also work nicely.

Serves 4

olive oil
1kg beef cheeks, trimmed and cut
   into bite-sized pieces
150g streaky bacon, cut into strips
2 garlic cloves
2 dried bay leaves
1 large carrot, peeled and
   finely chopped
1 onion, finely chopped
300ml dry red wine
2 tablespoons tomato purée
400g tinned chopped tomatoes
400g dried macaroni
300g wild mushrooms, washed
   and trimmed
leaves from a small bunch of flat-leaf
   parsley, chopped
Parmesan cheese for
   grating (optional)
sea salt and freshly ground black
   pepper

Preheat the oven to 160°C/Fan 140°C/Gas Mark 3.

Heat a good splash of olive oil in a large flameproof casserole or heavy-based ovenproof saucepan with a tight-fitting lid over a medium-high heat. Season the beef cheeks with salt and pepper then add to the casserole, in batches, and brown all over. Remove and set aside.

Add the bacon to the same pan and stir for a few minutes until it is nicely browned. Reduce the heat to medium, then add the garlic, bay leaves, carrot and onion, and stir for 5 minutes, or until the onion is softened but without colour. Add the wine and tomato purée, scraping the residue from the base of the pan, and stir for 2 minutes to cook out the paste. Return the beef cheeks to the pan with any juices and pour in the chopped tomatoes. Bring to the boil, then cover and place in the oven for 2 hours, or until the beef is meltingly tender and the sauce is rich and thick.

Remove the casserole from the oven and give everything a good stir. If the sauce looks too thick, add a splash of water. Re-cover the casserole and set aside for the meat to rest.

Bring a large pan of salted water to the boil. Add the macaroni and cook according to the packet instructions. When it's al dente, drain, reserving a small cup of the cooking liquid.

Meanwhile, heat a large sauté pan over a medium heat and add a splash of oil. Add the mushrooms, season, and fry, stirring, for 4–5 minutes until they are cooked through and lightly browned. Stir through the parsley.

Add the pasta to the casserole with the mushrooms, the cup of cooking water and a good splash of oil. Place over a medium heat and stir to combine. Let the mixture bubble for 2 minutes and season. Divide among individual bowls, grate over the Parmesan, if using, and serve.

Zganci

polenta with pancetta, herbs and sheep's cheese

A national dish of Croatia, *zganci* is a spartan and simple porridge-like, polenta-like mix made with nutty buckwheat flour, water and salt. Like Italian wet polenta it can be transformed into a food fit for kings. My recipe uses milk and stock as the base and finishes with fatty pancetta, herbs and finely grated sheep's cheese. The buckwheat flour is lightly toasted before adding to the liquid for a flavour boost.

This is great as a standalone first course or good to serve as an accompaniment to roast meat or a slow-cooked ragout or casserole. If you want to make this vegetarian, just swap the chicken stock for vegetable and replace the pancetta with wild mushrooms.

Serves 4 as a starter

350ml chicken or vegetable stock
  (fresh or homemade is best)
350ml whole milk
100g buckwheat flour
50g instant polenta
1 garlic clove, finely chopped
30g pecorino, or other sheep's
  cheese, grated
a handful of fresh oregano leaves
a handful of flat-leaf parsley
  leaves, chopped
50ml extra virgin olive oil, plus extra
  for drizzling
50g thinly sliced pancetta
sea salt and freshly ground black
  pepper

Pour the stock and milk into a large saucepan and season well. Bring to a boil, then turn down the heat and leave to simmer. Heat a large sauté pan over a medium heat. Add the buckwheat flour and use a wooden spoon to toss and stir the flour until it turns light brown – it will start to smell 'toasty'. Tip the flour out of the pan into a bowl and set aside to cool.

Whisk the buckwheat flour, polenta and garlic into the simmering milk mix, whisking until fully incorporated. Cook slowly for 25–30 minutes, whisking, until the mixture is smooth and thick – like a porridge or wet polenta. Whisk in half the pecorino, all the oregano and parsley leaves and the extra virgin olive oil.

Meanwhile, preheat a grill to medium-high heat.

Transfer the mixture to a flameproof serving dish. Drizzle with more extra virgin olive oil, scatter over the remaining cheese and top with the strips of pancetta. Place under the grill for 3–4 minutes until the pancetta is cooked and the cheese is brown. Serve at the table for everyone to help themselves.

Fritules

doughnuts scented with orange and hot chocolate sauce

Croatian doughnuts originate from the coastal region of Dalmatia. Like many traditional sweet recipes, they are especially popular at Christmas and Easter, but I think they should be enjoyed throughout the year – they are far too good just for holidays. I used rum to flavour the *fritule*, as that's what I had to hand, but they are traditionally flavoured with a Croatian liqueur called *loza*.

These are delicious served straight from the fryer and dusted with icing sugar, but here I've added a simple chocolate dipping sauce as it seemed the right thing to do! I think bitter chocolate works best with the hot orange-scented doughnuts.

Makes about 20;
the sauce makes about 500ml

500g plain white flour
60g golden caster sugar
7g sachet fast-action dried yeast
1 large free-range egg, beaten
1 teaspoon vanilla extract
1½ tablespoons light rum
grated zest and juice of 1
   unwaxed orange
200ml milk, lukewarm
60g raisins
rapeseed oil for deep-frying
icing sugar for dusting

For the hot chocolate sauce
200ml whole milk
40g unsalted butter, chopped
300g 70% dark chocolate

Mix the flour, sugar and yeast together in a large bowl and make a well in the centre. Add the egg, vanilla, rum and orange zest and juice, and stir well with a wooden spoon, then gradually stir in the milk, drawing in the flour from the side. A thick batter should start to form, then use a whisk to mix to make sure everything is well combined and that there are no lumps. Stir in the raisins and leave to rest for 30 minutes. You should have a batter with a dropping consistency – if it's a little thick, add a splash more milk.

Meanwhile, make the hot chocolate sauce. Heat the milk in a saucepan over a medium heat until hot, then stir in the butter and chocolate. Continue stirring over the heat until the chocolate and butter have melted, and the sauce is rich and glossy. Set aside and keep warm.

When you're ready to cook the doughnuts, heat enough oil for deep-frying in a deep-fat fryer or a large heavy-based saucepan until it reaches 180°C, or a piece of bread sizzles and turns golden. Line a bowl with kitchen paper and set aside.

Quickly drop teaspoonfuls of the batter in to the fryer without over-crowding, and fry for about 2 minutes until they are golden brown all over. Use a slotted spoon to transfer the doughnuts to the bowl.

Dust with icing sugar and serve with the hot chocolate sauce for dipping.

Greek Salad

This effortlessly simple salad, inspired by a wonderful taverna on the island of Zakynthos, goes really well with grilled meats and fish.

The key ingredients are olives – preferably unpitted Kalamata – good-quality, barrel-aged feta, ripe sweet tomatoes, cucumbers and red onions. I like to leave the feta in a big chunk on top, Zakynthos style, but you might prefer to crumble the cheese into the salad.

Serves 4

20 ripe sweet baby tomatoes, such as
    datterini or cherry vine, halved
1 small cucumber, roughly chopped
    into small pieces
1 small red onion, halved and very
    thinly sliced
12 salted capers, rinsed
a handful of unpitted Kalamata olives
16 tablespoons extra virgin olive oil,
    plus extra for drizzling
3 tablespoons red wine vinegar, such
    as cabernet sauvignon
a small handful of dill fronds
a small handful of mint leaves
60g piece of barrel-aged feta, drained
    and cut into chunky pieces
a pinch of dried chilli flakes
sea salt and freshly ground black
    pepper

Place the tomatoes, cucumber, onion, capers and olives together in a bowl, then season well. Add the oil and vinegar and gently mix so everything is well coated. Place the bowl in the fridge to marinate and chill for at least 10 minutes and up to 30 minutes. This salad should be served very cold to be refreshing.

Remove the salad from the fridge and toss in the fresh herbs, then divide among 4 bowls. Top each with a piece of feta, sprinkle over the chilli flakes, grind over some pepper and add a drizzle of extra virgin olive oil. Serve.

Roasted Carrots
with caraway seeds, mint and onion seeds

I like to make food notes on my travels so that I have a log of good things eaten to spark ideas to be developed when I'm back home. My scrawling from a recent visit to Greece highlighted this wonderful dish of roasted carrots enjoyed at an Athens taverna called Diogenes.

Serves 4

600g mixed carrots – I use a selection of orange, yellow and purple, scrubbed, trimmed, halved lengthways and then cut into bite-sized pieces
2 small red onions, quartered with the ends left intact
olive oil
2 teaspoons caraway seeds, lightly crushed
juice and grated zest of 1 unwaxed orange
leaves from 1 bunch of mint, shredded
a handful of flat-leaf parsley leaves, chopped
2 good splashes of extra virgin olive oil
2 teaspoons black onion seeds (nigella)
sea salt and freshly ground black pepper

Preheat the oven to 200°C/Fan 180°C/Gas Mark 6.

Place the carrots and onions in a roasting tray, drizzle with olive oil, sprinkle over half the caraway seeds and season. Roast for 35–40 minutes until the carrots are tender and caramelised.

Transfer the carrots and onions to a bowl and mix in the orange juice and zest and mint and parsley leaves, the extra virgin olive oil and the remaining caraway seeds. Gently mix it all through with your hands, then transfer to a large serving platter. Sprinkle over the onion seeds and serve.

Courgette and Feta Fritters
with preserved lemons, dill and mint

These fritters are as ubiquitous in Greek tavernas as moussaka. The best are spiked with pieces of salty-sour preserved lemons and a generous helping of fresh green herbs.

They are delicious with a sprinkle of sea salt, a squeeze of lemon and a yoghurt dip, or a bowl of aïoli (page 38 or shop bought) on the side is also good.

Makes about 16

3 very fresh courgettes (the heavier
   the better), coarsely grated
2 preserved lemons, deseeded and
   finely chopped
1 fresh red chilli, deseeded and
   finely chopped
1 large free-range egg, beaten
25g plain white flour
20g Parmesan cheese, finely grated
fronds from ½ bunch of dill, roughly
   chopped, plus extra for scattering
leaves from ½ bunch of mint, roughly
   chopped, plus extra for scattering
100g feta cheese, drained and
   patted dry
olive oil
lemon wedges, to serve
sea salt and freshly ground black
   pepper

Mix the courgettes, preserved lemons, chilli, egg, flour, cheese, dill and mint together in a bowl and season well. Scrunch it all up with your hands, then crumble in the feta and mix again.

You might have to cook these in batches, depending on the size of your pan. If so, preheat an oven on a low setting and line a baking tray with kitchen paper. Heat a large sauté pan over a medium heat, then add enough olive oil to cover the surface by 0.5cm. When it's hot, fry tablespoons of the mixture for 2–3 minutes on each side until they are golden brown and hot. Drain well on kitchen paper and keep hot until all the mixture is used.

Sprinkle the fritters with sea salt and fresh herbs and serve with lemon wedges for squeezing over.

Barbecued Prawns
on bay and rosemary skewers

This is a dish I made on holiday one year at our villa in Milos. The rosemary and bay branch skewers add a herby, aromatic perfume to the prawns as they grill. Look for particularly woody stalks on the herbs so that they can hold the weight of the prawns while grilling. Keep the heads on the prawns while they cook, then when they come off the grill, squeeze the sizzling head juices over the tails. You can also make this recipe using squid or scallops. These are delicious with good bread, such as Carinola (page 70) or Focaccia Barese (page 52).

Serves 4 as a starter

4 rosemary branches, needles
    removed from all but the ends
4 bay leaf branches, leaves reserved
24 raw head-on Atlantic or
    tiger prawns
olive oil
aïoli (page 38 or shop bought), to serve
sea salt and freshly ground black
    pepper

For the marinade
2 garlic cloves, finely chopped
1 fresh red chilli, deseeded and
    finely chopped
1 tablespoon extra virgin olive oil
2 teaspoons red wine vinegar, such as
    cabernet sauvignon
1 teaspoon clear honey
½ teaspoon chopped fresh rosemary
    needles (use the needles from
    the branches)

First make the marinade. Whisk the garlic, chilli, extra virgin olive oil, vinegar, honey and chopped rosemary together. Season with salt and pepper. Set aside.

To prepare the skewers, cut each rosemary and bay leaf branch roughly to 12cm or so, and sharpen the ends with a vegetable peeler to create a point.

Alternating the prawns with the reserved bay leaves, skewer 3 prawns onto each of the rosemary skewers and 3 prawns onto each bay skewer.

Place the skewers into a shallow non-metallic tray, spoon over three-quarters of the marinade and leave to marinate for 30 minutes.

Light a barbecue about 30 minutes before you want to cook so the coals turn ashen grey and are at the optimum grilling temperature. Position the grill above the coals so it gets very hot. Alternatively, heat a large ridged, cast-iron griddle pan to maximum.

Remove the skewers from the marinade and pat dry. Pour the marinade into a small saucepan and bring to the boil on the grill rack or on the hob.

When the marinade is boiling, drizzle the skewers in olive oil then place them on the grill, which you might need to do in batches, depending on the grill size. Cook the prawn skewers for 3 minutes on each side, or until cooked through and nicely charred. Transfer from the grill to a serving platter and drizzle over the reserved marinade while they are still hot. Serve with the aïoli.

Holiday Chips

I'm obsessed with the delicious chips you get in Greek tavernas and restaurants, known locally as *patatas tiganetes*. They are everything you could want from a fried potato. I think aïoli (page 38 or shop bought) is the perfect accompaniment.

Serves 4–6

4 Maris Piper potatoes, peeled and
    cut into 1cm chips
olive oil (not too spicy) for
    deep-frying
sea salt
dried oregano (optional)

Put the potatoes in a bowl of cold water to cover and leave for 1 hour. This is to remove the starch.

Heat just enough olive oil to cover the potatoes in a deep-fat fryer or heavy-based saucepan until about 150°C – a piece of bread will fizzle and slowly and steadily turn golden brown. (This is a lower temperature than you would use to fry in vegetable oil because of olive oil's lower flash point.)

Drain the potatoes and pat them completely dry. Carefully lower the potatoes into the oil and fry for 10–15 minutes until the chips are tender and golden brown – the potatoes will take on a golden hue from the oil. Cook in batches, if necessary, and keep hot in a low oven. Reheat the oil to the correct temperature between batches.

Use a slotted spoon to transfer the chips to kitchen paper to drain and sprinkle immediately with sea salt and dried oregano, if using. Serve.

Slow-cooked Beef Shin, Stifado Style
with fennel and toasted pistachios

The ancient beef dish *stifado* has Italian heritage, travelling to the Greek islands during the Middle Ages. The use of dried rather than fresh herbs in this dish is essential, giving authenticity and delicious flavours.

Stifado is made with lamb, pork, venison and rabbit, though I think beef produces the most robust version. Beef shin is the best cut for slow cooking and adds its own complexity to the finished dish. Serve with buttered noodles or rice.

Serves 4–6

1.5kg boneless beef shin, diced
500g shallots, peeled but left whole
2 small heads fennel, quartered
300ml dry red wine
3 tablespoons red wine vinegar, such as cabernet sauvignon
4 garlic cloves, sliced
3 dried bay leaves
2 teaspoons ground allspice
2 teaspoons dried oregano
1 teaspoon dried rosemary
1 teaspoon ground cloves
½ teaspoon ground nutmeg
olive oil
400g tinned chopped tomatoes
250ml water
2 tablespoons tomato purée
1 teaspoon light brown sugar
a handful of pistachio nuts, toasted and roughly chopped, to serve
extra virgin olive oil for drizzling
sea salt and freshly ground black pepper

Place the beef, shallots and fennel in a bowl, then add the wine, vinegar, garlic, bay, allspice, oregano, rosemary and ground cloves and nutmeg. Set aside for at least 4 hours or up to 24 hours.

Preheat the oven to 180°C/Fan 160°C/Gas Mark 4. Strain the liquid from the beef, shallots and fennel and reserve.

Pat the beef, shallots and fennel dry. Heat a good splash of olive oil in a large flameproof casserole over a medium heat. When it is hot, fry the shallots for 4–5 minutes until just browned all over, then use a slotted spoon to remove and set aside.

Add more oil to the casserole and fry the beef and fennel, in batches, until nicely browned. Return the shallots and any beef or fennel to the casserole with the reserved liquid, tomatoes, water, tomato purée and sugar. Give it all a good stir.

Cover the casserole and bring to a simmer, then transfer to the oven for 2½ hours, stirring halfway through. Remove from the oven and leave to rest for 30 minutes without uncovering.

To serve, adjust the seasoning, then sprinkle over the pistachios and drizzle with extra virgin olive oil.

Pork Belly Gyros and Tzatziki

Pork and lamb gyros are a popular street food snacks all over Greece and make the ultimate sandwich. I've added zingy sumac, oregano and charred shallot slices to the tzatziki, which add a sweet depth. I've included a small amount of *za'atar* in the dry rub for the pork belly. This is a mix of herbs and spices – typically dried oregano and thyme with sesame seeds and sumac – that is a backbone of much Middle Eastern cooking.

Makes 4

750g boneless, skinned pork belly
2 garlic cloves, finely chopped
1 tablespoon dried rosemary
1 tablespoon dried thyme
1 tablespoon cumin seeds, crushed
1 teaspoon *za'atar*
olive oil
¾ small cucumber, thinly sliced
2 tablespoons caster sugar
1 teaspoon sumac
2 heads baby gem lettuce,
    finely sliced
2 plum tomatoes, cored and
    roughly chopped
finely chopped rind of 2
    preserved lemons
4 pitta breads (page 154 or shop
    bought), halved and warmed
sea salt and freshly ground black
    pepper

For the tzatziki
olive oil
2 banana shallots, cut into
    0.3cm slices
250ml thick Greek yoghurt
¼ small cucumber, grated
juice of 1 lemon
a handful of fresh oregano leaves,
    roughly chopped
a handful of mint leaves,
    roughly chopped
a pinch of sumac

Preheat the oven to 150°C/Fan 130°C/Gas Mark 2.

Place the pork belly on a foil-lined baking tray. Mix the garlic, rosemary, thyme, cumin seeds, *za'atar*, a good splash of olive oil, a pinch of salt and a few grinds of pepper together in a bowl, then rub this all over the pork belly. Roast the pork for 50 minutes to cook through and tenderise the meat. Increase the oven temperature to 200°C/Fan 180°C/Gas Mark 6 and roast for a further 40 minutes to caramelise and crisp up the fat. Remove the pork belly from the oven and leave to rest and cool for 30 minutes, then cut into 1cm slices.

Meanwhile, make the tzatziki. Heat a splash of olive oil in a sauté pan over a medium-high heat. When it is hot, add the shallots and fry for 6–7 minutes until they are nicely charred and softened, stirring as you go. Remove them from the pan and leave to cool.

Stir the shallots, yoghurt, grated cucumber, lemon juice, oregano, mint and sumac together in a bowl. Season and chill until required.

About 10 minutes before you want to serve, mix the sliced cucumber, sugar, sumac and a pinch of salt together in a bowl, and leave to rest for 10 minutes. Add the lettuce, tomatoes and preserved lemon rinds, and toss together.

To assemble the sandwiches, stuff the pittas with pork belly, tzatziki and the cucumber-and-lettuce salad. Nothing more needed!

Clemence Street Moussaka

Moussaka, while mostly associated with Greece, has its roots in the Middle East where layers of aubergine, tomato and meat are baked and combined with fresh herbs, cheeses and spices. Eastern Europe also has a version that predates the Greek.

The Greek version, however, appeared in the 1920s, developed by the influential chef and cookery writer Nikolaos Tselementes, whose now globally renowned recipe contains Béchamel sauce, aubergines and a rich, cinnamon-spiced lamb ragout. This is my version, inspired by many wonderfully vivid and sparkling Greek holidays, now regularly enjoyed at our home in East London.

Serves 4

olive oil
3 medium or 2 large aubergines, cut
    lengthways into 0.5cm slices
a handful of panko breadcrumbs
1 large onion, finely chopped
4 garlic cloves, finely chopped
1½ teaspoons ground cinnamon
a handful of mint leaves, chopped,
    plus extra, to garnish
a handful of parsley, chopped
500g minced lamb
2 tablespoons tomato purée
200ml dry red wine
400g tinned chopped tomatoes
sea salt and freshly ground black
    pepper

For the sauce
500ml whole milk
60g butter, diced
60g plain white flour
50g *kefalotyri* or pecorino cheese,
    grated, plus extra to
    finish (optional)
2 large free-range eggs, beaten
a nutmeg for grating

Preheat the oven to 200°C/Fan 180°C/Gas Mark 6. Lightly oil as many baking sheets as you need to hold the aubergine slices in a single layer.

Place the aubergines on the baking sheets. Sprinkle with the breadcrumbs, drizzle over a little olive oil and season. Bake for about 20 minutes until they are soft, golden and tender. Do not turn off the oven when you take out the aubergines.

Meanwhile, heat a good splash of olive oil in a large frying pan over a medium-high heat. When it is hot, add the onions and fry, stirring occasionally, until they are softened but without colour. Add the garlic, cinnamon and half the mint leaves, and stir for a further couple of minutes.

Stir in the lamb, turn up the heat slightly and brown the lamb well, cooking until the mixture is quite dry. Stir in the tomato paste and wine and bring to a simmer, then add the tomatoes. Turn the heat down to low and leave to simmer for 30–40 minutes until most of the liquid has evaporated. Season well and stir in the parsley.

Make the sauce. Bring the milk to just below boiling in one pan and melt the butter in another saucepan over a medium-low heat. Stir the flour into the butter and continue stirring for 2 minutes, then gradually whisk in the hot milk, until you have a thick, smooth sauce. Add the cheese and stir until it melts. Take the pan off the heat and leave the it to cool slightly, then beat in the eggs, grate in nutmeg to taste and season with salt and pepper.

Arrange one-third of the aubergines on the base of an ovenproof serving dish, then top with half the lamb ragout. Repeat these layers, finishing off with a layer of aubergine and the sauce spooned over the top.

Place the dish on a baking sheet and transfer to the oven. Bake for about 45 minutes until bubbling and well browned. Set aside to cool for 30 minutes before serving. Sprinkle over extra cheese, if you want, and garnish with the remaining mint leaves.

Cephalonia-style Walnut Cake

I was first introduced to this well-known walnut cake on the wonderful Ionian island of Cephalonia. Refined and rustic at the same time, it has gentle spicing with the bitter edge of the walnuts offset by a citrusy syrup. It's no wonder that this is one of the most iconic puddings of Greece. It's addictive and delicious, with or without ice cream.

Makes 8–10 slices

250g unsalted butter, softened, plus extra for buttering the tin
200g caster sugar
360g plain white flour, plus extra for dusting the tin
4 large free-range eggs
200g shelled walnut halves, plus extra to finish
½ teaspoon ground cloves
1 tablespoon ground cinnamon
120g whole milk
1 tablespoon baking powder
a pinch of table salt
icing sugar, to finish
ice cream, to serve (optional)

For the syrup
400ml water
400g caster sugar
1 cinnamon stick
peeled zest of 1 unwaxed lemon

First make the syrup. Place the water, sugar, cinnamon stick and lemon zest in a small saucepan, and bring to the boil. Continue to boil for 3–4 minutes until the sugar dissolves and the mixture becomes syrupy. Turn off the heat and leave the syrup to cool.

Preheat the oven to 190°C/Fan 170°C/Gas Mark 5. Butter and flour a 22cm springform cake tin 10cm deep, then line the base with a piece of parchment cut to fit.

Using a stand mixer, with a beater attached, beat the butter and sugar on medium speed until light and fluffy. Beat in 30g of the flour, then beat in the eggs, one by one, until thoroughly mixed.

Place the walnuts and spices in a food processor and blitz to make rough, coarse crumbs – larger, rustic bits are great, as you want some texture in the cake. Transfer the nuts to the bowl, along with the remaining flour, the milk, baking powder and salt, and beat for 2 minutes to incorporate everything well. You'll have a thick batter. Transfer the batter to the tin and spread evenly.

Transfer the cake tin to the oven and bake for 50 minutes, or until the cake has risen and is a beautiful golden brown. A skewer inserted into the centre should come out clean. Remove the tin from the oven and place on a wire rack.

Remove the cinnamon stick and lemon zest from the pan of syrup. Use a skewer to make small holes all over the top of the cake, then pour over the syrup. Leave the cake for at least an hour to cool and to allow the syrup to be fully absorbed.

When ready to serve, remove the cake from the tin and peel off the lining paper. Dust with icing sugar and sprinkle over extra walnuts. Cut into slices and serve with a scoop of ice cream, if you like.

eastern shores

Turkey
Syria
Lebanon
Palestine
Egypt

If the countries that sit on the eastern shores of the Mediterranean are less commonly associated with the azure sea than their northern shore cousins, it is surely the common threads of olives and olive oil, lemons, nuts, tomatoes and fresh herbs that bind them so firmly together. So, too, the distinctive climate of long, hot summers followed by cool winters and sporadic intense winds – a climate that has a profound and specific influence on vegetation, wildlife and the dazzling shared food culture. Here are a few of my favourite eastern shore inspirations.

Levant feasts

I have my friend Kevin Gould to thank for introducing
me to the culinary splendours of this part of the
Mediterranean. A journalist of note and a food writer
of distinction, Kevin has long been a staunch advocate of
the food blessings in Turkey and across the eastern shores
of the Mediterranean. He spent many years travelling,
reporting and eating in the region long before it became
fashionable. Before I experienced the region's culinary
delights for myself, I looked forward to visiting his house in
Shepherd's Bush, London, where wonderful and expansive
feasts would be prepared for open house parties. Hungry
guests would be greeted by laden tables of delicious
preparations – perhaps braised and stuffed courgettes and
aubergines served with wild rice, or a slow-cooked sticky
shoulder of lamb fragrant with aromatic spices nestled next
to a vibrant fresh herb salsa. These formative meals inspired
me to venture forth to Turkey with strict instructions from
Kevin to go off-piste and head to Marmaris on the south
coast. It was, he told me, a place of great beauty and delicious
foods. And so it was. I was instantly hooked on Turkey and
on the eastern shores of the Mediterranean.

Sweet and sour

Though Syria, Lebanon, Israel, Palestine and Egypt have their own unique and separate food cultures, it is the things that they have in common that I find so fascinating and appealing. The freshness and textures of the salads, lightly spiked with spices such as cumin or sumac and given crunch with raw onions; the profusion of delicious vegetables; the abundance of fresh herbs often used as a base for salads – perhaps a simple mound of dressed mint leaves studded with tomatoes and olives; grilled meats and fish, smoky and burnished and salty outside but juicy within; charred or baked flatbreads lightly drizzled with olive oil or browned butter. But, above all this, it is the way in which the acidity from lemon and vinegar and the sweetness from the molasses and honey are combined in so many of the eastern shore dishes that I find so irresistible.

These sweet-sour flavour combinations are seriously addictive and most certainly one of my favourite things.

Smoke, spice and street food

Egypt has a wonderfully rich culinary tapestry and culture. The markets and food stalls blaze bright in a riot of colour, aromas, noise and frenetic activity. So many dishes feeding so many needs. *Fuul*, the Egyptian breakfast staple for the early risers, is picked up from stalls to be eaten in the street on the way to work. Beloved by Egyptians, *fuul* is essentially a spiced fava bean pancake sprinkled with a dukkah spice mix and stuffed into a pitta – sometimes fried or scrambled eggs are added.

Around lunchtime the *hawashi* makes its appearance. Spiced lamb or beef is cooked with green chilli, cinnamon and allspice, finished with fresh mint and coriander, then stuffed into flatbread, folded and baked in super-hot wood ovens until charred and crisp. The cooks then remove them from the oven to cool, to be stacked and cut into slices to take away – the more discerning might add mayonnaise or a *zhoug*-type sauce to spice it up further.

And in Turkey – Istanbul, to be specific – the ultimate lunch sandwich can be found on the banks of the Bosporus. Hugely popular with locals and tourists, as the queues testify, are the grilled mackerel sandwiches: hot and smoky from a barbecue, stuffed into a thick sandwich with some sort of mouth-puckering pickled cucumber or tomato salad to offset the always perfectly fresh and delicious mackerel. My version is on page 128.

Staff meals and the best grilled chicken

I have been privileged over the years to employ and work with very many chefs from many cultures. And, thus, our restaurant staff meals were a joy and a place for all of us to learn. My chefs from Syria and Palestine would often pull out all the stops and produce feasts of multiple dishes layered with unfamiliar flavour combinations. Everything was delicious and vibrant, and everything was eaten.

My most memorable dishes were those that involved spatchcocked grilled chicken, enriched with charred skin and layered with multiple, contrasting flavours of sweet honey, fresh herbs and sour sumac. This was truly a favourite eastern shore chicken dish, and you can enjoy my version on page 167.

Sweet pancakes (pastry) and even sweeter coffee

Fiteer is a kind of Egyptian filo-based sweet pizza that is heated through on an outdoor grill before being drenched in honey, icing sugar and syrup infused with rosewater. It's intensely sweet and dangerously addictive. If paired with a shot of heavy-duty Egyptian coffee served with equal amounts of strong coffee to sugar – you'll be supercharged for the rest of the day.

Another super-sweet treat to have with coffee is the brittle-like pistachio and sea salt caramel that you can buy in various shaped shards to munch as you walk down the street or to take home. The super-bitter Egyptian coffee is a great contrast to the deep, rich caramel flavour. My recipe is on page 186.

Pides

with toasted sesame seeds and molasses

If you've been to Turkey or eaten at a Turkish restaurant, you'll know any number of variations on this wonderful Turkish flatbread. It can be found stuffed with rich meat or cheese fillings, flavoured with fresh herbs and pungent spices and / or ripe sweet tomatoes. It is in all probability the Eastern precursor to pizza. I like my *pides* unadorned, very hot, ready to be torn and shared. Once you've got the bread technique nailed to perfection, you'll have the option to top or not to top!

A past sous chef of mine was brought up in Istanbul and used to make *pides* for our staff dinners; he loved showing the young chefs how his mum used to make it. The family secret, though not a secret anymore, is plenty of stretching and pulling, plus a brush of sticky sweet molasses just before serving.

Makes 2 large pides

250g plain white flour, sifted, plus
    extra for dusting
250g strong white flour, sifted
7g sachet fast-action dried yeast
1 teaspoon clear honey
pinch of table salt
400ml lukewarm water
olive oil for greasing the bowl
1 large free-range egg yolk, whisked
    with a splash of olive oil
a handful of sesame seeds
50ml pomegranate or date molasses
sea salt, to finish

Put both flours, the yeast, honey and table salt in a large mixing bowl. Make a well in the centre and add the lukewarm water, then bring together using your hands. Transfer the dough to a floured work surface and knead for a few minutes until you have a smooth dough. Shape into a ball, place in the washed and greased bowl, and cover with a tea towel. Set aside in a warm spot for an hour, or until doubled in size.

Turn out the risen dough onto a floured surface, knock back and cut into 2 equal portions. Flatten each portion, then place them on separate sheets of baking parchment. Re-cover with the tea towel and set aside in a warm place for 10 minutes for the gluten in the flour to relax.

Still on the parchment, use greased fingers to press and stretch each piece into a thin rectangle, about 30 x 10cm. Cover again with the towel and leave in a warm spot for 15 minutes.

Meanwhile, preheat the oven to 240°C/Fan 220°C/Gas Mark 9, with 2 large baking sheets inside.

Brush the top of each piece of dough with the egg-and-oil wash. Use your greased fingers to make indentations in the dough, then sprinkle with sesame seeds. Remove the baking sheets from the oven and carefully slide a *pide*, still on the paper, onto each sheet.

Bake for 10 minutes, or until golden brown and puffed up. Immediately brush each *pide* with half the molasses, sprinkle with sea salt and set aside on a wire rack to cool. Serve.

Chaban
shepherds' salad

Translated as 'the shepherd', this salad would traditionally have been prepared for lunch by hungry shepherds and farmers using pickings from their own crops, gathered on the way back to their homes – usually cucumbers, tomatoes, peppers and olives. Feel free, however, to add anything you like into the mix. I love spring onions, finely chopped radishes and bags of fresh herbs.

This simple salad is touched with culinary magic through the addition of citrusy sumac and a gorgeous dressing infused with toasted coriander and cumin seeds. Pair it with salty feta cheese and warm *pides* (page 120).

Serves 4–6

16 radishes, trimmed and finely
   chopped, with the leaves reserved
12 green olives, pitted and halved
4 spring onions, finely chopped
3 large ripe vine tomatoes, cored,
   halved and finely chopped
2 small green peppers, deseeded and
   finely chopped
1 red pepper, deseeded and
   finely chopped
1 small, heavy cucumber, halved
   lengthways, seeds removed and
   finely chopped
leaves from 4 fresh thyme sprigs
leaves from 1 small bunch of mint
leaves from ½ small bunch of
   flat-leaf parsley
1 teaspoon sumac, to finish
sea salt and freshly ground black
   pepper

For the dressing
1 teaspoon coriander seeds,
   lightly crushed
1 teaspoon cumin seeds,
   lightly crushed
3 tablespoons extra virgin olive oil
1 tablespoon red wine vinegar

First make the dressing. Heat a sauté pan over a medium heat. Add the coriander and cumin seeds and toast, stirring constantly, for a minute or so to release their oils and until they become fragrant. Immediately transfer them to a bowl. Add the olive oil and vinegar, season with salt and pepper and whisk together. Set aside.

Place the radishes, olives, spring onions, tomatoes, green and red peppers and cucumber in a large bowl. Add the herbs and radish leaves with salt and pepper and toss together. Add the dressing and toss again.

Transfer to a large serving bowl or individual bowls and sprinkle with sumac. It's ready to serve.

Braised Courgettes
stuffed with spiced wild rice and served with tomato sauce

This is a vibrant, summer plate inspired by a lovely lunch I once enjoyed in Izmir. I love slowly cooking courgettes in the oven to intensify their natural sweetness and, as here, they make a great vessel or 'boat' for a nutty, spiced rice filling. A fresh tomato sauce always works well with roasted courgettes and I've added a warm note of cinnamon. You can add grilled halloumi to this if you fancy, but in all honesty it's deliciously fresh and vibrant just as it is.

The ubiquitous spice mix *ras el hanout* is found all across the southern and eastern Mediterranean, and used in many savoury dishes, often rubbed into meat or fish, or used as an excellent flavouring in sauces. As with many spice blends of the region, there is no definitive recipe, and, traditionally, every family has a unique mix of spices to make up their own blend, but they'll all have a fiery warmth and beautifully perfumed aroma. You can easily buy *ras el hanout* in supermarkets and Middle Eastern shops.

Although I suggest serving this dish hot, both the courgettes and sauce are equally good served at room temperature with a salad alongside.

Serves 4; the sauce makes about 500ml

160g wild rice, washed
olive oil
1 large red onion, finely chopped
1 teaspoon *ras el hanout*
leaves from 4 or 5 fresh thyme sprigs,
    plus extra, to garnish
5 large courgettes
80g green olives, pitted and halved
a handful of flat-leaf parsley,
    roughly chopped
50g pine nuts, toasted, to garnish
sea salt and freshly ground black
    pepper

For the tomato sauce
50g butter
3 garlic cloves, thinly sliced
½ teaspoon ground cinnamon
½ teaspoon dried chilli flakes
750g plum vine tomatoes,
    roughly chopped
leaves from 4 or 5 fresh thyme sprigs

First make the tomato sauce. Melt the butter in a saucepan over a medium heat. When it's sizzling, add the garlic, cinnamon and chilli flakes. Once the garlic starts to colour, add the tomatoes, thyme leaves and salt and pepper, then simmer, uncovered, stirring often to avoid the sauce catching and burning, for 30 minutes, or until it is thick and rich. Blitz until smooth in a blender or food processor, or use a stick blender. Set aside.

Meanwhile, bring 350ml of water with a generous pinch of salt to the boil in a large saucepan. Add the wild rice and return the water to the boil, then lower the heat and leave to simmer until all the water has been absorbed. Turn off the heat, cover the pan and leave the rice to steam for a few minutes. Drain well and set aside.

Heat a good splash of olive oil in a large sauté pan over a medium heat. When it's hot, add the onion, *ras el hanout* and thyme leaves with salt and pepper, and leave the onion to sweat, stirring occasionally, while you prepare the courgettes.

...continued on page 124

Cut the 4 largest courgettes in half lengthways, then scoop out the flesh with a teaspoon, leaving an edge of about 0.5cm thick. Chop the courgette flesh, then finely dice the remaining courgette. Add the chopped flesh and diced courgette to the onion and cook slowly, stirring occasionally, for 8 minutes, or until softened but without colour.

Preheat the oven to 220°C/Fan 200°C/Gas Mark 7.

Place the hollowed courgette halves upright in a roasting tray, drizzle with olive oil and season with salt and pepper. Transfer to the oven and roast for 15 minutes, or until tender.

Mix the cooked rice with the onion and courgette mixture, the olives and half the parsley, then season. Divide equally among the courgette halves and drizzle with olive oil. Return to the oven for a further 15–20 minutes until the courgettes are just tender. Reheat the tomato sauce, if necessary.

To serve, sprinkle the courgettes with toasted pine nuts, the remaining parsley leaves and the extra thyme leaves. Serve with the warm sauce.

Leek Fritters
and whipped yoghurt flavoured with caramelised lemon

These delicious and ridiculously moreish fritters are traditionally served piping hot fresh from the oven as a starter or as part of a mezze. The incredible yoghurt dip is a revelation and can be used to serve alongside anything you fancy. The caramelised lemon juices are so much more than the sum of their parts, adding a deep, sweet-sour flavour to the whipped yoghurt. I love it.

Serves 4

olive oil
25g unsalted butter
3 leeks, washed, trimmed and
   thinly sliced
2 large free-range eggs
50g crème fraîche
100g self-raising white flour
1 teaspoon baking powder
150g good-quality feta, drained
   and crumbled
a handful of tarragon leaves,
   finely chopped
a handful of flat-leaf parsley leaves,
   finely chopped
milk (optional)
extra virgin olive oil, to serve
sea salt and freshly ground black
   pepper

For the dip
1 lemon, halved
150g Greek yoghurt
2 tablespoons double cream
1 teaspoon sumac

Preheat the oven to 180°C/Fan 160°C/Gas Mark 4.

Heat a good splash of olive oil in a sauté pan over a medium heat. When it is hot, add the butter and stir until it melts. Add the leeks and cook slowly, stirring often, for 10 minutes, or until softened but without colour. Set aside.

In a mixing bowl, whisk the eggs with the crème fraîche until light and airy, then stir in the flour and baking powder to make the batter.

Fold in the leeks, feta and tarragon and parsley leaves, and season well. You should have a consistency that will slowly drop from the spoon. If it is too dry, add a dash of milk; too wet, add a pinch of flour. Set aside until ready to serve.

Wipe out the pan with crumpled kitchen paper and heat a layer of oil about 2cm deep until a little of the batter sizzles instantly on impact with the oil. Use an oiled tablespoon to drop 4 separate dollops of batter into the pan. Push each one with the back of the spoon until you have small patties. Fry for about 3 minutes until they are beautifully golden brown and crisp, then carefully turn them over and continue frying until golden brown on the other side. When the fritters are fried, transfer them to a baking tray and continue until all the batter is used.

When all the fritters have been fried, place them in the oven for 15 minutes, or until they are piping hot.

Meanwhile, make the dip. Heat a small sauté pan over a medium-high heat. Add the lemon halves, cut side down, and dry-fry for 5 minutes to caramelise the juices and soften the flesh. Turn off the heat and set aside to cool.

Whisk the yoghurt with the cream, add the sumac and season to taste. Squeeze the juice from the caramelised lemon (avoiding any seeds) into the yoghurt and stir together.

Serve the fritters sprinkled with sea salt and extra virgin olive oil drizzled over with the dip alongside.

Istanbul-style Fish Sandwich

If you've been to Istanbul, you'll have probably seen these sandwiches flying out from street vendors by the banks of the Bosporus. Traditionally they are made with smoky mackerel, grilled over charcoal and wood, the skins crisp and blistered to just a few degrees short of burnt. Watching the men work away in the wafting smoke, dramatically grilling and stuffing the sandwiches, is a memorable sight not to be missed.

These best-ever fish sandwiches work perfectly with cooling yoghurt, crisp lettuce leaves and sour pickled onions to offset the charred fish. This is a great recipe for barbecues and picnics.

Makes 4

1 red onion, sliced into thin rings
1 teaspoon caster sugar
2 tablespoons sweet white wine
    vinegar, such as chardonnay
4 large fresh mackerel fillets,
    pin bones removed and skins
    lightly scored
olive oil
1 lemon, halved
sea salt and freshly ground black
    pepper

For the sauce
3 tablespoons Greek yoghurt
1 teaspoon pomegranate molasses
½ teaspoon sumac
1 tablespoon olive oil

To serve
1 head baby gem lettuce,
    leaves separated
a handful of fresh dill fronds
a handful of mint leaves
4 ciabatta or other crusty rolls,
    cut through horizontally

Place the onions in a non-metallic bowl. Add the sugar and a good pinch of salt, then stir in the vinegar. Toss together and leave for 30 minutes or so to pickle.

If you are using a barbecue, light the coals about 30 minutes before you want to cook so they turn ashen grey and are at the optimum grilling temperature. Position the grill above the coals so it gets very hot. Alternatively, heat a large ridged, cast-iron griddle pan to maximum.

Meanwhile, make the sauce. Mix the yoghurt with the molasses and sumac, then season well and whisk in the olive oil. Cover and chill until ready to serve.

Rub the mackerel fillets all over with olive oil and season well. Place them skin side down on the hot grill rack and grill for 3–4 minutes to crisp and char the skins. Flip the fillets over and continue grilling for 1–2 minutes on the underside until just cooked through – the flesh will feel firm and be opaque. Remove from the rack and squeeze over some lemon juice.

Just before serving, toss the lettuce leaves with the dill fronds and mint leaves, a splash of olive oil and onion pickling liquor to taste.

To serve, spread the rolls with the yoghurt sauce on each cut side. Pile the lettuce-and-herb mix on the bottom halves, then add the mackerel and the pickled onions and top with the roll lid. I like to skewer these with wooden cocktail sticks to serve.

Zahter-flavoured Slow-cooked Lamb
with broad beans and greens

All across the Mediterranean lamb is revered and embraced. When cooked very slowly, it becomes soft and unctuous, with the fat rendered through the meat to keep it moist. In this recipe, a marinade of citrus zest and spices infuses the lamb, giving a perfumed deliciousness to the cooked meat.

This is inspired by the spring, using vibrant green broad beans that go brilliantly with lamb, and *zahter*, a Turkish herb that you can buy preserved in olive oil in Middle Eastern food shops and from online suppliers – it has similarities to rosemary, oregano and thyme. If you can't find it, fresh rosemary and thyme leaves tossed in olive oil with a splash of lemon juice are a very good alternative.

Serves 4

1 lamb shoulder on the bone,
　about 1.1kg
olive oil
100ml pomegranate molasses
2 handfuls of seasonal greens, such
　as Swiss chard, curly kale or large
　spinach leaves, picked over
　and rinsed
200g fresh or defrosted broad beans,
　picked from their grey 'jackets'
1½ tablespoons *zahter* in olive oil
　(see introduction, above), drained,
　to garnish
sea salt and freshly ground black
　pepper

For the marinade
1 garlic clove, peeled
2 teaspoons ground cinnamon
2 teaspoons sweet smoked paprika
grated zest of 1 unwaxed lemon
grated zest of 1 unwaxed orange
needles from 3 fresh rosemary sprigs
leaves from 3 fresh thyme sprigs

First make the marinade. Place the garlic, cinnamon, paprika and lemon and orange zests in a pestle and mortar and roughly pound together to make a thick paste.

Place the lamb in a bowl, rub all over with olive oil and season. Rub the marinade all over the lamb and scatter over the rosemary needles and the thyme leaves. Leave the lamb in the fridge to marinate for at least 3 hours or up to 24 hours.

When you are ready to cook, preheat the oven to 170°C/Fan 150°C/Gas Mark 3.

Heat enough olive oil to cover the base of a large flameproof casserole over a medium heat. When it is hot, add the lamb and brown on all sides. Leave to cook for a few minutes, then cover with the lid or foil, place in the oven and roast for 2½ hours, or until the meat is very tender.

Remove the casserole from the oven, uncover and leave the lamb to cool for a good 30–40 minutes.

Remove the lamb from the cooking liquid, then carefully spoon off and discard the excess fat. Stir the molasses in to the juices remaining in the casserole, return it to the heat and bring the liquid to the boil. Lower the heat and leave to simmer, stirring occasionally, until a thick sauce forms. Tear the lamb off the bone into chunks and add to the sauce.

Meanwhile, heat a splash of oil in a large sauté pan over a medium heat. When it is hot, add the greens with salt and pepper. Cook, stirring, until the greens begin to wilt, then add the broad beans and continue stirring for a further 2–3 minutes until everything is tender.

To serve, transfer the greens and beans to a large serving plate and arrange the lamb pieces over the top with some of the sauce. Sprinkle over the *zahter*.

Meatballs Roasted with Tomatoes
and rose harissa

Alaçati is a beautiful seaside town close to Izmir on the west coast of Turkey with a long wine-making tradition and excellent restaurants. My wife and I have holidayed there several times on the recommendation of my good mate Kevin Gould. Kevin used to write a column for *The Guardian* called 'Eat Like a Local', where he would travel to non-touristy locations known for great food culture and eat what locals ate. Alaçati was top of his list, and this is my homage to the Alaçati meatball. I serve these with freshly boiled rice, steamed couscous or just-baked pitta breads (page 154).

Serves 4

olive oil
1 red onion, finely chopped
2 garlic cloves, finely chopped
1 tablespoon *ras el hanout*
½ teaspoon ground cinnamon
a large handful of flat-leaf parsley,
    stalks and leaves chopped separately
500g minced lamb
300ml chicken stock (fresh or
    homemade is best)
600ml passata
2 tablespoons rose harissa paste
4 tablespoons Greek yoghurt, to serve
a handful of dill fronds, chopped,
    to garnish
a handful of mint leaves, chopped,
    to garnish
sea salt and freshly ground black
    pepper

Heat a splash of olive oil in an ovenproof saucepan with a tight-fitting lid over a medium heat. When it is hot, add the onion and fry, stirring, for about 10 minutes until it is beginning to soften. Add the garlic and *ras el hanout* and stir for 2 minutes. Transfer half the onion to a large mixing bowl and leave to cool. Put the other half on a plate and set aside.

Meanwhile, preheat the oven to 200°C/Fan 180°C/Gas Mark 6.

Add the cinnamon, chopped parsley stalks and lamb to the onion in the bowl. Season and use your hands to mix everything together. Divide the mixture into 12 equal portions and roll into balls.

Heat another splash of oil in the pan. Add as many meatballs as will fit and sauté them for 6 minutes, or until browned all over. Remove from the pan and set aside. Continue until all the meatballs are browned, adding extra oil to the pan, if necessary.

Return the remaining onion to the pan with the stock, passata and rose harissa. Heat until the liquids start to simmer, then add the meatballs, stirring to coat them well. Cover and transfer to the oven for 10 minutes.

Uncover the pan and return it to the oven for a further 10 minutes, or until the meatballs are cooked through and the sauce is deep, rich and thickened. Set aside for 10 minutes to let the flavours develop and blend.

To serve, spoon over the yoghurt and sprinkle over the dill, mint and parsley leaves.

Spiced Lentils
with squash and chicken

I can only take a little credit for this recipe. The real credit must go to its creator, Suliman, one of my talented cooks at The Thomas Cubitt Pub, in London. It first appeared at a staff food day, and when I tasted it I was blown away. It was not only delicious and vibrant, but was a great way to use leftover roasted or grilled chicken, giving it new life. It was handed down to Suliman by his aunty who used to make *perde pilav* (veiled rice) for grand weddings. *Perde pilav* is an elaborate, spiced chicken pilaf baked in a decorative crust. There was always extra chicken to use up and this was the family's favourite solution. It is completely delicious and ready in just 40 minutes.

I suggest you use butternut squash, or another heavy squash, for the best flavour, but pumpkin works just as well when it is in season.

Serves 4

1 tablespoon coriander seeds
olive oil
2 carrots, peeled and roughly chopped
1 onion, finely chopped
200g peeled butternut squash or
    pumpkin, deseeded and cut into
    bite-sized chunks
2 garlic cloves, crushed
½ teaspoon dried chilli flakes
125g dried green lentils, rinsed
600ml chicken or vegetable stock
    (fresh or homemade is best)
2 tablespoons tomato purée
400g leftover roasted chicken, skin
    removed and shredded
100g curly kale or other seasonal
    greens, rinsed and chopped
juice of 1 lemon
a handful of mint leaves, chopped
a handful of flat-leaf parsley
    leaves, chopped
Aleppo chilli flakes, to garnish
sea salt and freshly ground black
    pepper

Heat a large, deep saucepan over a medium heat. Add the coriander seeds and toast for a few minutes, stirring, until fragrant. Immediately transfer to a pestle and mortar or a spice grinder and grind to a rough powder.

In the same pan, heat a splash of olive oil over a medium heat. When it is hot, add the carrots, onion and ground coriander, and sweat for 5 minutes, or until the onion is softened but without colour. Add the squash, garlic and chilli flakes, and cook gently, stirring occasionally, for 2–3 minutes.

Add the lentils and continue stirring for a further minute. Stir in the stock and tomato purée and bring to the boil. Reduce the heat and leave to simmer, uncovered, for 35 minutes, or until the lentils and squash are tender.

Stir in the chicken, kale, lemon juice and mint and parsley leaves. Season and continue simmering for 10 minutes, uncovered, or until the lentils are fully cooked and the kale has wilted. Serve, sprinkled liberally with Aleppo chilli flakes.

Flourless Bitter Chocolate Torte
flavoured with coffee, orange and cardamom

There used to be a bakery in Istanbul called Pastel, just off the chaos of the main street, Bebek. Here you'd find refined cakes and pastries straddling both the eastern and the western influences of this wonderfully cosmopolitan city. French and European-style delicacies flavoured with exotic aromatics and spicing shared shelves with more traditional Turkish bakes, such as baklava and *revani* (semolina cakes).

This cake is inspired by one I enjoyed from Pastel. It's a flourless torte that has been in my personal recipe book for years. I always have a version on the go at the restaurants. It's easy to make, surprisingly light and very delicious.

Here I've added my favourite Turkish-inspired flavours that work well with the dark chocolate. Serve with Greek yoghurt and some lightly poached fruit, such as apricots or plums, or the roasted peaches on page 138.

Makes 8–10 slices

300g 70% dark chocolate, cut
   into pieces
225g salted butter, diced
100ml warm espresso coffee, or 2
   teaspoons espresso coffee granules
   dissolved in 100ml hot water
7 large free-range eggs
175ml water
225g caster sugar
5 green cardamom pods,
   lightly crushed
grated zest of 1 large unwaxed orange
a pinch of table salt

Preheat the oven to 160°C/Fan 140°C/Gas Mark 3. Grease and line a 23cm round springform tin 10cm deep.

Melt the chocolate and butter in a bain-marie or a heatproof bowl set over a saucepan of hot water, then stir in the coffee. When everything is incorporated, set aside and keep warm.

Crack the eggs into a bowl and, using a hand-held electric mixer, whisk on high speed to aerate the eggs.

Place the water in a small saucepan over a high heat and bring to the boil. Add the sugar and cardamom pods, stirring to dissolve the sugar, then boil for 2 minutes to create a flavoured syrup. Leave to cool slightly, then pour very slowly into the eggs, whisking constantly.

After the syrup is incorporated and the eggs are fluffy, gradually fold in the chocolate mix, orange zest and the salt until fully incorporated.

Pour the mix into the cake tin and smooth the surface. Transfer to the oven and bake for 40 minutes, or until the cake is set around the edge with a slight wobble in the centre.

Remove the tin from the oven, transfer to a wire rack and cool to room temperature. Cover with cling film and chill for at least 2 hours, or up to 24 hours, before removing from the tin and slicing. A hot knife is best for this.

Labneh Cheesecake
with roasted peaches, honey and cardamom

The fresh, citrusy labneh in this cheesecake is the perfect backdrop for the luscious, sweet peaches spiced with sultry, aromatic cardamom. One of my favourite cheesecakes, this is inspired by a version I used to buy for breakfast when on holiday in Alaçati from a lovely neighbourhood bakery. I loved the way the bakers used filo pastry to make an ultra-crisp and light base reminiscent of baklava when blended with the nuts.

I'd suggest making this over two days to give yourself time to ensure that the cake is perfectly set. The fruits can be changed seasonally – use plums, apricots or nectarines, for example.

Makes 8–10 slices

For the base
90g unsalted butter, melted, plus
    extra for buttering the baking tin
olive oil, for greasing
5 sheets filo pastry
60g shelled pistachio nuts
40g walnut halves
50g caster sugar
1 tablespoon plain white flour
seeds from 10 green cardamom
    pods, crushed
a pinch of table salt

For the filling
400g labneh
400g ricotta, strained
210g caster sugar
100g full-fat mascarpone
a pinch of table salt
2 large free-range eggs, plus 3 large
    free-range egg yolks
1½ tablespoons cornflour
1 tablespoon orange blossom water
finely grated zest of ½
    unwaxed orange

Heat the oven to 180°C/Fan 160°C/Gas Mark 4. Butter and line a 23cm round springform cake tin 10cm deep and lightly grease a baking sheet with olive oil.

First make the base. Lay out one sheet of filo on a work surface. Measure out one third of the melted butter, which will be used to brush the filo layers, and reserve the remaining butter for later use.

Brush the filo sheet with butter and then lay another sheet on top and brush again. Repeat until you have a stack of buttered filo sheets.

Place the filo stack on the greased baking sheet and bake for 20–25 minutes until crispy and golden brown. Remove from the oven, transfer the pastry to a wire rack and set aside to cool. Then break the filo sheets into large shards.

Blitz the filo pastry in a blender or food processor until fine crumbs form, then transfer to a bowl. Blitz the pistachios and walnuts to fine crumbs, then stir them in to the filo crumbs with the caster sugar, flour, cardamom seeds and salt. Stir in the reserved melted butter, then transfer to the springform tin and press across the base and onto the side.

Transfer to the oven and bake for 10 minutes, or until golden brown. Place on a wire rack and set aside while you make the filling.

For the topping

4 tablespoons orange juice
3 tablespoons clear honey
1 tablespoon orange blossom water
seeds from 8 green cardamom
   pods, crushed
400g ripe yellow or white peaches,
   stones removed and each cut
   into 8 wedges
a handful of mint leaves, to decorate

To make the filling, place the labneh, ricotta, caster sugar, mascarpone cheese and salt in the cleaned food processor bowl and blitz to combine. Add the whole eggs and yolks, cornflour, orange blossom water and the orange zest, and blitz again for a minute or two. Pour the mixture into the springform tin and smooth the surface.

Transfer the tin to the oven and bake for 1 hour, or until the edge is a rich golden brown, but the centre still has a wobble. Remove the tin from the oven and leave the cheesecake to cool for an hour before placing it in the fridge to set for at least 3 hours, but ideally overnight.

To make the topping, preheat the oven to 220°C/Fan 200°C/Gas Mark 7. Place the orange juice, honey, orange blossom water and crushed cardamom seeds in a small saucepan over a high heat, stirring to dissolve the honey, and boil until reduced by about half. Place the peaches in a roasting tray or ovenproof dish, pour over half the syrup and transfer to the oven. Bake for 10 minutes, or until the peaches are just softened. Remove from the oven and leave to cool.

An hour before serving, release the cake from the tin and transfer to a serving plate. Top the cake with the roasted peaches, spoon over the remaining syrup and scatter over the mint. Serve.

Chard, Potato and Chilli Saffron Omelettes
with yoghurt

This is my version of the Syrian-style breakfast omelette known as *ejjeh*. It's not just for breakfast, though; I'll happily make these for dinner with a fresh salad or cut them into slices to serve as part of a mezze. The saffron and yolks impart a vibrant yellow to the omelette base, which I find irresistible alongside the greens and fresh herbs.

Be creative – vary the herbs with coriander and thyme and use kale or black cabbage in place of the chard. I've also made this with chopped leafy radishes using the same quantities.

Makes 4

50g new potatoes, peeled and cut into
　1cm dice
200ml water
a pinch of saffron threads
350g Swiss or rainbow chard, washed
　and chopped
1 fresh red chilli, deseeded and
　finely sliced
1 garlic clove, crushed
juice of 1 lemon
5 large free-range eggs
60ml whole milk
a small handful each of chives, dill
　fronds and flat-leaf parsley leaves,
　all roughly chopped
olive oil
100g Greek yoghurt
sea salt and freshly ground black
　pepper

Place the potatoes, water, saffron and a good pinch of salt in a saucepan and bring to the boil. Lower the heat and simmer until the potatoes are just tender. Add the chard and continue simmering, uncovered, for a further 10 minutes, or until the potatoes and chard are tender and the water has evaporated. Remove from the heat and add the chilli, garlic and lemon juice. Set aside until cooled to room temperature.

When you're ready to cook, preheat the oven to 200°C/Fan 180°C/ Gas Mark 6 and lightly grease a baking sheet. Whisk the eggs, milk and herbs together, then season well with salt and pepper.

Heat a large non-stick sauté pan over a medium-high heat. When it is hot, add a good splash of olive oil and pour in one-quarter of the egg mix to make a thin, round omelette. As soon as it is set, transfer to a plate to cool, then repeat the process to make 3 more omelettes using all the egg mix.

To assemble, spread half of each omelette with one quarter of the yoghurt, then divide the chard and potato mixture equally among them. Fold each omelette over the covered half, then fold along the middle to get a fan-shaped case, allowing the filling to show on the open side.

Transfer the omelettes to the baking sheet and place in the oven for about 10 minutes until piping hot. Serve immediately.

Lavash

This staple crisp bread is perfect as part of a mezze for dips, pickles, cheeses or simply drizzled with the freshest extra virgin olive oil. Vary the toppings as you see fit. I always add a sprinkle of sea salt and then vary the flavourings, such as fennel, cumin, sesame and poppy seeds, chilli flakes and / or *za'atar*.

Serves 4–6; makes 4 large pieces

180g strong white flour, plus extra
    for rolling out
15g unsalted butter, softened
½ teaspoon table salt
a pinch of caster sugar
about 70ml water
olive oil
1 egg, beaten, for an egg wash
sea salt, fennel seeds, sesame seeds
    and chilli flakes – or whatever
    flavourings you fancy, to finish

Mix the flour, butter, salt and sugar together in a mixing bowl. Make a well in the centre, then gradually add the water and mix to form a firm dough. Do not knead. Cover the bowl with cling film and transfer to a fridge for an hour to rest.

Meanwhile, preheat the oven to 190°C/Fan 170°C/Gas Mark 5 with 2 large baking sheets inside.

Cut the dough into 4 pieces. Roll out each piece on a lightly floured work surface until very thin – turn and rotate as you roll to get an even thickness. Carefully remove the baking sheets from the oven and lightly brush with olive oil.

Transfer the dough to the hot baking sheets. Brush each piece of dough with the beaten egg, then sprinkle with salt, fennel and sesame seeds and chilli flakes – or any other seeds and spices you like.

Bake for 10 minutes, or until each bread is crisp and golden brown. Transfer them to a wire rack and leave to cool completely before serving.

Beetroot and Radish Salad
with walnuts and pomegranate seeds

I love the crunch and fresh pepperiness of radishes. They are delicious in a salad with sweet earthy beetroots, pomegranate and bitter greens. Try to buy radishes in a bunch as their leaves are great tossed through the salad for an extra mustardy kick. This salad is a stunner and has the most seductive look of deep reds and vibrant pinks. For time and efficiency, I buy cooked beetroots for this salad.

Serves 4

200g cooked beetroots
1 bunch of leafy radishes, halved
    lengthways with the leaves
    removed, washed and reserved
1 bunch of watercress sprigs,
    stalks trimmed
seeds from ½ pomegranate
½ teaspoon sumac
2 tablespoons red wine vinegar, such
    as cabernet sauvignon
extra virgin olive oil
a handful of walnut halves,
    lightly toasted
sea salt and freshly ground black
    pepper

Cut the beetroots into bite-sized pieces, which can be halves or quarters, depending on the size.

Place the beetroots, radishes and their leaves, the watercress sprigs and pomegranate seeds in a mixing bowl. Season well and sprinkle in the sumac. Toss well, then add the vinegar and a couple of splashes of extra virgin olive oil. Mix again, add the walnuts and serve immediately.

Roasted Fish
with a chilli-spiced stuffing

I love to roast whole fish in the summer and serve them with this classic Syrian spiced stuffing – a mixture of onions or shallots, hazelnuts, chopped coriander and a little chilli. It's delicious straight from the oven as it is, or the fish can be left to sit in its juices for a few hours, then eaten at room temperature. Sea bass and sea bream work well, but you can also cook a single larger fish to share, such as a turbot or brill.

Serves 4

2 whole fish, such as sea bass or sea bream, cleaned and gutted
1 lemon, halved
olive oil
Beetroot and Radish Salad (page 143), to serve (optional)
sea salt and freshly ground black pepper

For the stuffing and topping
50g skinned hazelnuts, finely chopped
4 garlic cloves, finely chopped
2 fresh red chillies, finely chopped
1 small onion, finely chopped
½ teaspoon ground cardamom
½ teaspoon ground coriander
½ teaspoon ground cumin
extra virgin olive oil
1 bunch of coriander, leaves and stalks roughly chopped
½ lemon, sliced

To make the stuffing, mix the hazelnuts, garlic, chillies, onion, ground spices and salt and pepper together with a good splash of extra virgin olive oil.

Divide half this mix between the fish cavities. Mix half the chopped coriander into the remaining stuffing and reserve.

Squeeze the lemon juice over the fish, drizzle with olive oil and season well. Leave in the fridge to marinate for 15 minutes.

Meanwhile, preheat the oven to 200°C/Fan 180°C/Gas Mark 6.

Transfer the fish to a roasting tray, pat the remaining stuffing mix over the top, then arrange lemon slices on top. Place in the oven and roast for 30–35 minutes until the fish are fully cooked through and the flesh is opaque and juicy. Finish with the remaining coriander and serve with the beetroot salad.

Roasted Spiced Lamb
with roasted tomatoes and tahini sauce

I love this dish. Essentially, it's a baked lamb meat patty or a sort of reassembled kebab with plenty of pungent spicing, fresh coriander and sticky slow-roasted tomatoes baked over the meat to ensure ultimate juiciness through the cooking process. Traditionally this type of dish is cooked for large family gatherings and parties in a huge iron skillet in an outdoor communal oven.

The tahini sauce is quite different to the more pedestrian versions readily available. It has a lovely sweet-and-sour kick, thanks to the tangy pomegranate molasses. It's a Syrian culinary classic.

Serves 4; sauce makes about 150ml

8 plum vine tomatoes, halved
   across the centre
olive oil
1 tablespoon sweet white wine
   vinegar, such as chardonnay
450g minced lamb
2 green chillies, deseeded and
   thinly sliced
1 onion, finely chopped
1 tablespoon tomato purée
2 teaspoons cumin seeds, crushed
1 teaspoon coriander seeds, crushed
1 teaspoon ground cinnamon
1 teaspoon sweet smoked paprika
leaves from 1 bunch of
   coriander, chopped
sea salt and freshly ground black
   pepper

For the tahini sauce
120ml tahini
1 garlic clove, finely chopped
2 tablespoons Greek yoghurt
1 tablespoon pomegranate molasses
juice of ½ lemon
2 tablespoons water

Place the tomatoes in a roasting tray, cut side up, and season well with salt and pepper. Drizzle with olive oil and spoon over the vinegar. Place in the oven and roast for 30 minutes, or until the tomatoes are starting to caramelise, the juices are bubbling and they have begun to shrink. Set aside.

Meanwhile, place the minced lamb in a bowl. Add the green chillies, onion, tomato purée, cumin and coriander seeds, cinnamon, paprika and one-third of the chopped coriander, and season. Mix everything together so all the flavourings are distributed.

Press the mixture into a thin layer in a 20cm round flameproof dish, then top with the tomato halves. Place in the oven and roast for 25 minutes, or until the meat is cooked through and the tomatoes are fully roasted and caramelised. You can flash this under a hot grill to finish caramelising the tomatoes, if you want. Leave to rest for 10 minutes before serving.

To make the sauce, blitz the tahini, garlic, yoghurt, molasses, lemon juice, water and one-third of the remaining chopped coriander with salt and pepper in a blender or food processor to make a smooth green sauce.

Sprinkle the remaining chopped coriander over the tomatoes and lamb and serve with the tahini sauce on the side.

Quince and Honey Tart

Quince and honey is an ambrosial match made in heaven and an historical flavour combination dating back to Roman times. This tart is baked with a frangipane-like mixture – the almond butter paste is enriched with yoghurt that adds a nice tang to the tart. It's a neat method that is used frequently in Syrian and Middle Eastern baking.

I've suggested cooking the quinces in wine which, though not authentic to the Middle East, imparts a depth of flavour and brings colour. You can, however, replace the wine with a mix of stock syrup and pomegranate molasses.

I like to use a rectangular tin for this, but a round one will work just as well.

Serves 10–12

800ml water
250ml dry red wine
200ml clear honey
100g caster sugar
3 star anise
3 quinces, peeled, halved lengthways, cored, deseeded with the seeds reserved and the flesh thinly sliced
juice of ½ lemon
olive oil for greasing the tin

For the pastry
250g plain white flour, plus extra for rolling out
150g cold unsalted butter, diced
2 tablespoons icing sugar
1 egg yolk
4 tablespoons iced water

For the yoghurt and almond filling
350g Greek yoghurt
200g ground almonds
160g unsalted butter, melted and cooled
110g whole milk
75g caster sugar
1 large free-range egg, plus one extra white
1½ tablespoons plain white flour

Place the water, wine, honey, sugar, star anise and reserved quince seeds in a saucepan over a medium heat, stirring until the honey and sugar dissolve. Add the quinces and simmer over a low heat for 50 minutes, or until they are soft and tender.

Leave the quinces to cool in the syrup, then use a slotted spoon to remove and set aside. Strain the poaching liquid into another pan and bring to a boil. Continue boiling until the liquid reduces by half and forms a thickish syrup.

While the syrup is reducing, make the pastry. Put the flour, butter and icing sugar in a food processor, and blitz until the mixture resembles fine crumbs. Add the egg yolk and water and pulse until the mixture comes together in a smooth ball. Shape into a disc, wrap in cling film and chill for at least 30 minutes.

Grease a 34 x 11cm loose-bottomed, fluted tart tin, or use a 26cm round tart tin.

Roll out the pastry on a lightly floured work surface until about 0.5cm thick. Use it to line the bottom and side of the tin, leaving excess pastry overhanging the edge. Chill for 10 minutes.

Meanwhile, preheat the oven to 200°C/Fan 180°C/Gas Mark 6.

Trim the pastry edge and prick the base with a fork. Line the pastry case with baking parchment and weigh down with baking beans or rice. Place the tin on a baking sheet and bake for 20 minutes, or until the pastry case is set and lightly browned. Remove the paper and beans, then bake for a further 10 minutes.

Reduce the oven temperature to 180°C/Fan 160°C/Gas Mark 4.

To make the filling, place all the ingredients in a bowl and beat to combine. Pour into the pastry case and smooth the surface, then arrange the quince slices on top. Bake for 40 minutes, or until the filling is set and the pastry is crisp and golden brown.

Increase the oven temperature to 200°C/Fan 180°C/Gas Mark 6. Brush the quince with some of the reserved syrup and return to the oven for 10 minutes, or until the quinces are caramelised and sticky. Transfer to a wire rack to cool for 20 minutes before drizzling with more syrup. Leave to cool completely before removing from the tart tin and slicing to serve.

Date Cake
with warm dark caramel sauce

Though not typical of traditional Syrian sweet treats, this cake brings with it strong Syrian influences both in the ingredients and flavours. It is typical though of a new wave of bakeries and pastry shops popping up all over Damascus.

The baking culture in Syria is profound, both commercially and domestically, and it's still not unusual for a household to bake bread or sweets daily.

The key to this cake is the inclusion of toffee-like Medjool dates that give flavour, texture and moisture. Also, the caramel – I use 50/50 white caster and dark brown soft sugar to create a really deep, bittersweet caramel. Not for the faint hearted!

If you can't get mulberries, blackberries make a very acceptable alternative.

Makes 6–8 slices;
sauce makes about 350ml

200g Medjool dates, pitted
225ml boiling water
125ml vegetable oil, plus extra for
    greasing the tin
2 large free-range eggs
50g dark brown soft sugar
2½ tablespoons whole milk
1 teaspoon vanilla extract
250g plain white flour
1 teaspoon baking powder
1 teaspoon bicarbonate of soda
1 teaspoon ground cinnamon
mulberries or blackberries, to serve
whipped cream, to serve

For the dark caramel sauce
100g dark brown soft sugar
100g caster sugar
3 tablespoons unsalted
    butter, chopped
125ml double cream
½ teaspoon sea salt

Place the dates in the bowl of a standing mixer, fitted with a beating attachment, or a food processor, pour over the boiling water and leave to soak for 15 minutes. The dates should be completely covered.

Meanwhile, preheat the oven to 200°C/Fan 180°C/Gas Mark 6. Grease and line a 20cm springform cake tin 10cm deep.

After the dates have soaked, beat them until they are roughly puréed, but not completely smooth. Add the eggs, oil, brown sugar, milk and vanilla extract and beat for 3 minutes until well combined and fluffy. Use a spatula to transfer this mixture to a large mixing bowl.

Sift over the flour, baking powder, bicarbonate of soda and ground cinnamon, then fold the dry ingredients into the date and egg mixture.

Pour the batter into the tin and smooth the surface. Bake for 30–35 minutes until a skewer inserted into the centre of the cake comes out clean. Transfer to a wire rack to cool for 30 minutes before removing the tin and peeling off the paper.

While the cake is baking, make the dark caramel sauce. Put both sugars in a large non-stick sauté pan over a medium heat and leave until they melt and start to bubble. Do not stir the sugar at this stage or it will crystallise. Add the butter and swirl this into the caramel until it melts and the sauce is glossy.

Stir the caramel with a wooden spoon until the butter is blended, then stir in the cream. Continue simmering the caramel for 2–3 minutes to thicken. Turn off the heat and stir in the salt. Keep warm until ready to serve.

To serve, cut the cake into desired portions and spoon over the caramel sauce. Finish with the berries and then the cream and serve any extra sauce for adding at the table.

Sweet-and-sour Aubergine Confit

Sweet-and-sour flavours are typical of Lebanese and Middle Eastern cuisines in general. They are a legacy of inventive Arab cooks who would create dishes with honey and citrus to both preserve and also to add a mouth-puckering tang to help alleviate the sweltering heat.

This unusual – but delicious – 'pickle' is excellent when included as part of a mezze plate or in a sandwich with a soft cheese, such as feta, curd, ricotta or burrata. The confit can also be added into rice along with dried chilli flakes and a handful of basil leaves. The oil is good for adding to salad as part of a dressing. I always have a jar of this incredibly versatile pickle knocking about in my fridge at home.

Serves 8 or more

2 large aubergines, quartered
   lengthways with the flesh scored
250ml extra virgin olive oil, plus
   extra as needed
65ml red wine vinegar, such as
   cabernet sauvignon
1 tablespoon caster sugar
4 fresh bay leaves
3 fresh thyme sprigs
sea salt and freshly ground black
   pepper

Sprinkle sea salt over the cut sides of the aubergines and leave for up to an hour maximum to disgorge – you are essentially extracting moisture and bitterness. Wipe off the excess with a damp cloth.

Meanwhile, preheat the oven to 180°C/Fan 160°C/Gas Mark 4.

Transfer the aubergine to a roasting tray. Sprinkle over the olive oil, vinegar and sugar, then scatter with the bay leaves and thyme sprigs. Transfer to the oven and roast the aubergines for about an hour until they are very tender. Depending on your oven, it might take a little longer. You should be able to 'cut' the aubergines with a spoon.

Remove the tray from the oven and set aside to cool completely.

Transfer the aubergines and any oil remaining in the roasting tray to jars and cover with airtight lids. Transfer to the fridge and leave to marinate for at least 24 hours before using. They will last in the oil for up to 2 weeks if left unopened in the fridge and covered with extra olive oil once opened.

To serve, return to room temperature, then remove the aubergines from the oil and serve as you wish.

Fresh Pitta Breads

This ubiquitous bread is of ancient heritage, possibly prehistoric, though its exact origin is uncertain. Traditionally pitta breads are baked at a very high heat so the water content turns to steam, puffing the breads to create billowy pockets. These homemade ones are easy to make – just have faith in heat and air! Serve with harissa or zhoug, or wrap them around freshly grilled kebabs. These also freeze extremely well.

Makes 10

2 teaspoons fast-action dried
    yeast, or 20g fresh yeast
400–500ml lukewarm water,
    depending on the yeast
    you've used
1 teaspoon sugar, plus a pinch
    extra if using dried yeast
500g strong white flour, plus extra
    for dusting
1½ teaspoons table salt
2 tablespoons olive oil

If using dried yeast, dissolve it in 100ml lukewarm water with a pinch of sugar and set aside for 10 minutes, or until frothy. Mix the flour, salt and 1 teaspoon sugar together in the bowl of a stand mixer, with the dough hook attached. If using fresh yeast, crumble it straight in; if using dried yeast, make a well in the centre and add the yeast liquid.

Now pour in 400ml of lukewarm water, bit by bit, mixing on medium speed. Continue mixing and slowly adding the water until the dough is smooth and elastic. The exact amount of water you need will depend on whether you are using fresh or dried yeast and how absorbent your flour is, so don't add it all at once. Now add the oil and continue mixing and kneading until the dough is silky smooth.

Cover the bowl with cling film and leave at room temperature for an hour, or until doubled in size. If you want to bake the next day, transfer the bowl to the fridge and leave overnight. Before you carry on with the recipe, remove the bowl from the fridge and leave the dough for 30 minutes, or until it is room temperature.

Turn out the risen dough onto a floured surface and knock back. Cut it into 10 equal pieces, rolling each piece between your palms to make a ball. Place the balls on a floured surface, cover with a tea towel and leave to rest for 20–30 minutes until the dough rises again and they are puffy. Meanwhile, place one or two heavy baking sheets, depending on their size, in the oven and set the temperature to maximum heat.

Lightly sprinkle flour over the dough balls and roll each out to about the size of a starter plate, about 0.5cm thick. Set aside until all are rolled, then dust again with flour. Working quite quickly, transfer the flattened pieces of dough to the baking sheet and quickly return to the oven – using a floured spatula is the best way to do this. Depending on your oven size and your baking sheets, you will probably have to bake in batches.

The pittas will bake and puff up in 3–4 minutes, but don't let them colour. Remove them immediately from the oven and stack them in piles, covered with the tea towel, to stop them drying out.

Fried Spiced Potatoes
with red peppers, garlic and coriander

I think this is a delicious, flavoursome way to cook potatoes. You can turn up the heat as high as you wish with extra chilli flakes. The fresh chilli gives less heat here, but with more pepper flavour.

The subtle, comforting heat of these potatoes makes them a great accompaniment to grilled fish and lamb dishes. You can also serve them with a cooling spoonful of yoghurt or labneh dolloped on top or even some crumbled feta and mint.

Serves 4

1kg Charlotte or pink fir potatoes, peeled and cut into 2cm chunks
olive oil
5 garlic cloves, crushed
2 red peppers, cored, deseeded and cut into 1cm dice
1 fresh red chilli, deseeded and finely sliced
1 teaspoon coriander seeds, lightly crushed
½ teaspoon dried red chilli flakes
a handful of coriander leaves, chopped
grated zest of 1 unwaxed lemon
1 tablespoon squeezed lemon juice
sea salt and freshly ground black pepper

Preheat the oven to 240°C/Fan 220°C/Gas Mark 9, and bring a large saucepan of salted water to the boil. Put the potatoes into the boiling water and boil until they are just tender – you should be able to slide a knife in easily. Drain well and dry.

Mix the potatoes with a good splash of olive oil, season with salt and pepper and spread out in a single layer on a large roasting tray lined with kitchen foil. Place in the oven to roast for 10 minutes. Stir in the garlic, red peppers, fresh red chilli, coriander seeds and dried chilli flakes. Return to the oven and roast for a further 20 minutes, stirring occasionally. Add half the fresh coriander and continue roasting for 10 minutes, or until the potatoes are nicely browned and caramelised.

Remove the potatoes from the oven and transfer to a bowl. Adjust the salt and pepper, if necessary, then stir in the lemon zest and juice and the remaining fresh coriander. Serve.

Seven-spice Falafels
(the real deal)

Some years back I had a restaurant in Soho, London. After the lunch service I would head out to the Berwick Street market and buy a falafel wrap from the brilliant Jerusalem Falafel. The stall was very theatrical, presented as a live production kitchen. Hungry lunchtime customers could watch the mix being made, shaped, fried and wrapped in a homemade flatbread while their hunger pains grew. The long queues were testament to how good these relatively simple, rustic broad bean and chickpea balls were. I had to get the recipe. In the end, though, a falafel is only as good as the chickpeas they are made from and the spice mix used to flavour them. I've been to Lebanon and eaten a number of authentic falafels, but nothing quite beats this version, by way of Soho.

Makes 24

250g dried, split skinless broad beans
150g dried chickpeas
6 spring onions, thinly sliced
5 garlic cloves, crushed
1½ teaspoons Lebanese seven-spice
　mix (*bahrat*)
1 teaspoon ground coriander
1 teaspoon ground cumin
1 teaspoon table salt
leaves from a large bunch of
　coriander, roughly chopped
1 small bunch of flat-leaf parsley,
　leaves and stalks roughly chopped
rapeseed oil
½ teaspoon baking powder
4 tablespoons sesame seeds
sea salt

To serve
pitta breads (page 154 or shop bought)
Greek yoghurt
mixed salad ingredients
lemon wedges

Soak the broad beans and chickpeas in separate bowls of cold water to cover overnight. The next day, drain them well, keeping them separate. Tip both onto a separate tea towel to dry.

Put all the broad beans and half the chickpeas into a food processor and blitz until smooth. Add the spring onions, garlic, Lebanese spice mix, the ground coriander and cumin and table salt, and blitz again until well mixed. Add the remaining chickpeas, fresh coriander and parsley, and pulse until chopped and well combined, but not puréed – it should still be coarse.

Heat a splash of oil in a small pan over a high heat and fry a teaspoon of the mixture to check the seasoning. Add more salt and / or spices, if necessary. Stir in the baking powder, then cover the mixture with cling film and chill for 30–60 minutes.

Roll the mixture into 24 equal balls, then press into flattish balls, about 4cm across. Toss in sesame seeds to coat all over.

Heat about 5cm oil in a deep, heavy-based saucepan to 170°C – use a thermometer to get it right, but if you don't have one, a cube of bread should sizzle and turn golden. Fry the falafel in batches until golden brown, then drain well on kitchen towels and sprinkle with sea salt. Check the oil temperature between batches so it doesn't drop.

Serve with pitta breads, yoghurt, salad and lemon wedges for squeezing over.

Pear, Radish and Watercress Salad
with orange blossom dressing and pistachios

This is a dish I recreated at home after an intensive research trip to Tripoli. Back in my kitchen I replaced bitter wild purslane with peppery watercress and prickly pears with pears roasted with honey. The pistachios and orange blossom were non-negotiable and make this unusual and exotic salad taste authentic. It's a favourite of mine and one I prepare all year round. It's a dish that seems to straddle the seasons, appearing perhaps as part of a dinner feast or with some soft white cheese, grilled meat or just with a slice of grilled goat's cheese popped on top. Use pears that can stand up to some heat, such as a Comice or William.

Serves 4

2 pears, quartered lengthways
   and cored
2 teaspoons olive oil
1 tablespoon clear honey
16 long radishes, trimmed and
   halved lengthways
1 large bunch of watercress sprigs,
   stalks trimmed
a handful of dill fronds
40g shelled green pistachio nuts,
   roughly chopped, to serve
sea salt and freshly ground black
   pepper

For the orange blossom dressing
3 tablespoons extra virgin olive oil
1 tablespoon orange blossom water
1 tablespoon red wine vinegar, such
   as cabernet sauvignon

Preheat the oven to 200°C/Fan 180°C/Gas Mark 6.

Toss the pear pieces with olive oil and season with salt and pepper. Place in a roasting tray and roast for 20 minutes, or until softened and caramelised. Remove from the oven, drizzle with the honey and set aside to cool completely.

Meanwhile, make the dressing. Whisk the extra virgin olive oil, orange blossom water and vinegar together. Season with salt and pepper.

Transfer the pears to a bowl and spoon over half the dressing. Mix and press the pears a little to lightly break the edges, which helps them absorb the dressing. Set aside for 10 minutes.

Add the radishes, watercress, dill fronds and the remaining dressing, and season. Mix well and transfer to a serving bowl or individual bowls. Sprinkle over the pistachios and serve.

Fig Pavlova
with cinnamon meringue and almond cream

This is a real showstopper. Layers of crisp and fudgy meringue, praline cream scented with cinnamon, and juicy, ripe fresh figs, all stacked into a glorious sweet sandwich, oozing with the sultry flavours of the Lebanon. I made this recipe for a friend's wedding some time back, each table getting a pavlova to share, served family style. It was a great success.

Use the best black figs in season. Their juices should almost be bursting out of the skins. When they are at their best these glorious Mediterranean fruits need little in the way of embellishment. But I'm afraid I can't resist them when served in a decadent pavlova.

Serves 10–12

40g flaked almonds
50g 70% dark chocolate, chopped
50ml clear honey
600g fresh black figs, cut into
    thin slices

For the cinnamon meringue
130g large free-range egg whites
130g caster sugar
130g dark muscovado sugar
2 teaspoons ground cinnamon

For the almond cream
50g flaked almonds
80g caster sugar
2 tablespoons water
400g mascarpone
200ml double cream

Preheat the oven to 140°C/Fan 120°C/ Gas Mark 1. Place a sheet of baking parchment on a baking sheet and lightly draw a 34cm circle – this is to guide you for positioning the meringue.

To make the meringue, half fill a saucepan with water and bring to a simmer. Select a heatproof bowl that will fit over the pan without the bottom of the bowl touching the water. Place the egg whites and both sugars in the bowl and whisk by hand to combine. Place the bowl over the simmering water and whisk the egg whites for about 6 minutes until they are frothy and the sugar melts. Transfer this meringue to the bowl of a stand mixer, fitted with a beating attachment, and whisk on high speed for about 5 minutes until it is stiff and glossy. Or, remove the bowl from the heat and use a hand-held mixer to whisk until the meringue is stiff and glossy. Whisk in the cinnamon.

Spread the meringue inside the drawn circle, creating a nest by making the sides a little higher than the centre. Place the baking sheet in the oven and bake the meringue for 3 hours. Switch off the oven, but leave the meringues inside until they are completely cool – this will take about 2 hours. Do not open the door during this time. Once cool, remove from the oven and set aside.

Meanwhile, reheat the oven to 200°C/Fan 180°C/Gas Mark 6.

Toast all the almonds (90g in total) by spreading them out on a baking sheet and toast for 7–8 minutes, stirring occasionally, or until golden brown. Remove from the oven, divide into 2 portions – 40g for the pavlova, 50g for the almond cream. Set aside and leave to cool.

...continued on page 160

Wash and dry the bowl you placed over simmering water and set aside.

After the meringue has cooled for 2 hours, bring another pan of water to the simmer. Place the chocolate into the washed bowl and place it over the simmering water, making sure the base of the bowl does not touch the water. Stir until the chocolate melts. Leave to cool a little, then brush the chocolate inside the meringue, leaving the top and side without. Set aside again for an hour or so to let the chocolate set.

To make the almond cream, first make an almond praline. Place the 50g toasted almonds on a baking sheet lined with baking parchment and set aside. Place the sugar and water into a small saucepan over a medium-low heat, stirring until the sugar melts. Increase the heat and boil, swirling the pan, until a dark golden-brown caramel forms. Pour this caramel over the nuts and leave to cool completely. Transfer the praline to a food processor or blender and blitz until you achieve fine crumbs.

Just before you are ready to serve, place the blitzed praline in a large bowl with the mascarpone and cream and whisk until stiff peaks form. It won't take long – so don't overwhisk.

When you are ready to assemble, warm the honey. Spoon the almond cream into the centre of the meringue and top with the fresh figs. Stir the remaining almonds into the honey, then spoon these over the figs. The pavlova is now ready to serve.

Zhoug

Zhoug is an incredibly popular and versatile 'hot sauce', very popular in Palestine, Israel and across the Middle East. Use it on anything you fancy to give a tasty kick.

Makes about 200ml

1 bunch of coriander, leaves and stalks roughly chopped
1 bunch of flat-leaf parsley, leaves and stalks coarsely chopped
100ml extra virgin olive oil, plus extra to cover
2 garlic cloves, ground in a pestle and mortar
1 fresh red chilli, stem removed and coarsely chopped
1 teaspoon cumin seeds
½ teaspoon ground cloves
juice of 1 lemon
sea salt and freshly ground black pepper

Place the coriander and parsley in a blender or food processor with the extra virgin olive oil, garlic, chilli, cumin seeds, ground cloves and lemon juice. Blend to a coarse purée and season with salt and pepper.

Transfer to a jar with enough extra virgin olive oil to cover and seal with an airtight lid. The sauce will keep for up to 2 months in the fridge. Just keep it topped up with oil each time you use.

Tomato and Red Onion Salad

Here's the freshest of salads, ideal as a foil for rich grilled meat and fish dishes. It's the kind of salad you see all over the region. A salad that proudly uses the best seasonal ingredients bathed with a sharp, citrusy dressing to accompany a lamb or chicken shawarma. I like to use curly parsley in this as it adds a gentle herbaceous pepperiness to the salad.

Serves 4

600g seasonal tomatoes – a mix of
    colours and sizes is best – halved,
    cored and thinly sliced widthways
2 small red onions, halved and
    thinly sliced
leaves from 2 large handfuls of
    curly parsley
sea salt and freshly ground black
    pepper

For the dressing
½ teaspoon cumin seeds,
    lightly crushed
50ml extra virgin olive oil
1 tablespoon red wine vinegar, such
    as cabernet sauvignon
a pinch of caster sugar
juice of ½ lemon

Place the tomatoes and onions in a bowl and season with salt and pepper. Toss together and leave for a few minutes at room temperature.

Meanwhile, make the dressing. Heat a sauté pan over a medium-high heat. Add the cumin seeds and lightly toast until they become fragrant. Immediately transfer the seeds to a small bowl, add the extra virgin olive oil, vinegar, sugar and lemon juice, and season with salt and pepper. Whisk together.

Toss the parsley leaves through the tomatoes, drizzle with the dressing and gently mix through. Transfer the salad to individual dishes and serve.

Fried Eggs and Saffron and Cumin-spiced Potatoes
with shatta

Shatta is to be found on every Palestinian table to impart a fiery hit to any dishes in need of a boost. I especially love it for breakfast with eggs, potatoes and a spiced butter – a great way to kick-start the weekend after a busy working week. You can go red or green – it's the chillies that dictate this, and for breakfast mine's red. You'll need to plan ahead, as the *shatta* takes about three days to ferment. Once made, however, it can be stored in an airtight container in the fridge for a few months.

Serves 4; the shatta makes about 225g

400g new potatoes, scrubbed and
   cut into thin slices
olive oil
125g unsalted butter, chopped
pinch of saffron threads, soaked in
   a splash of lukewarm water
4 large free-range eggs
½ teaspoon cumin seeds,
   lightly crushed
sea salt and freshly ground black
   pepper

For the shatta

300g green or fresh red chillies,
   trimmed and thinly sliced – include
   the seeds
1½ tablespoons sea salt
4 tablespoons sweet white vinegar,
   such as muscatel or chardonnay
juice of ½ lemon
extra virgin olive oil to cover

First make the *shatta*. Place the chillies and salt in a non-metallic bowl and mix well. Cover with cling film and leave in the fridge for 3 days.

On the third day, drain the chillies. Place them in a blender or small food processor and pulse until a coarse paste forms. Add the vinegar and lemon juice and pulse again. Transfer to a sterilised jar. Add enough olive oil to cover, seal and keep in the fridge for up to 2 months. Be sure to top up the olive oil whenever you use.

Place the potatoes in a saucepan with enough salted water to cover and bring to the boil. Boil for 2 minutes to blanch, then drain and set aside.

Heat a good splash of olive oil in a large sauté pan over a low-medium heat. When it is hot, add the potatoes with salt and pepper and stir for 2–3 minutes until they start to colour. Add the butter and the soaked saffron with the soaking liquid. When the butter foams, crack in the eggs. Season and sprinkle over the cumin seeds.

Cook for 2–3 minutes, basting the eggs with the foaming saffron-and-cumin-infused butter, until they are nicely coloured and hot, but still with runny yolks. Some crispiness around the edge of the whites is nice, but that's me.

Turn off the heat. Divide the eggs and potatoes equally among 4 plates and serve with *shatta* on the side.

Spatchcocked Chicken
flavoured with sumac, harissa, honey, dukkah and dill

Spatchcocking allows the chicken to be cooked quickly and evenly, and is perfectly suited to cooking on a barbecue. The sumac in the marinade really elevates this dish, adding its own unique citrus spice to the rich, charred chicken. Popular throughout the Mediterranean, this ruby-red ground spice is made from dried berries, and you'll find it in larger supermarkets or Middle Eastern shops.

Serves 4–6

1 free-range chicken, 2kg
dukkah (page 187 or shop bought)
   to serve
fronds from 1 bunch of dill, to serve

For the marinade
grated zest and juice of 1 large
   unwaxed orange
3 tablespoons clear honey
2 tablespoons harissa (page 200 or
   shop bought)
2 teaspoons sumac
extra virgin olive oil

First make the marinade. Mix the orange zest and juice, honey, harissa, sumac and a good splash of extra virgin olive oil together, then set aside.

To spatchcock the chicken, place it breast-side up on a chopping board. Using a sharp pair of kitchen shears, snip off and discard the wing tips and leg knuckles. Turn the chicken breast-side down, and starting at the parson's nose (fleshy end of the rump), cut along one side of the backbone to the neck. Repeat on the other side of the backbone, then remove and discard the bone. Turn the chicken back over and, with the heel of both hands, press down firmly along the centre. You'll hear the wishbone crack and the chicken should flatten out. Point the thighs inwards and, using a sharp knife, score a few slices in the flesh. Transfer to a baking tray and pour the marinade over the chicken, rubbing it well into the cuts and gaps. Leave in the fridge for at least 2 hours to marinate.

If you're using the barbecue, light it about 30 minutes before you want to cook so the coals turn ashen grey and are at the optimum grilling temperature. Position the grill 20cm above the coals so it gets very hot. (Alternatively, preheat the oven to 240°C/Fan 220°C/Gas Mark 9.)

Place the chicken skin side down on the barbecue rack and grill for 20 minutes before turning and cooking for a further 20 minutes. Repeat this process once again, or until the skin is nicely charred and caramelised and the flesh is cooked through – the juices should run clear when you pierce the thickest part of the thigh. (If you are roasting the chicken, place it skin side up directly on an oven rack, with a roasting tray lined with kitchen foil underneath, and roast for 25 minutes, or until the skin is golden brown and crisp and the juices run clear.)

Once cooked, remove the chicken from the grill or oven and spoon over any cooking juices. Leave to rest for 15 minutes before cutting into pieces. Serve with some dukkah spooned over and an abundant scattering of fresh dill.

Knafeh

with cheese, pistachios and orange blossom honey syrup

This is a Palestinian institution, served all over the Middle East as a celebration cake. I love the combination of the very sweet syrup and the slightly salty white cheese, and this is one of my favourite cakes to search out as soon as I arrive in the Middle East. Here I've used a mix of ricotta, feta and mozzarella cheese, which work very well as an alternative to traditional Palestinian cheeses.

Kataifi pastry, which has a straw-like structure, is ideal for absorbing syrups and is the key to the recipe's success and authenticity. Middle Eastern shops should stock it or be able to get it for you, or you can order online.

Enjoy with a cup of rose-scented tea and your senses will whisk you away to the cafés of the Middle East.

Serves 6–8

200g unsalted butter, melted, plus
    extra for buttering the tin
375g *kataifi* pastry (see introduction,
    above), defrosted and pulled apart
200g grated mozzarella cheese
100g ricotta
150g feta cheese, drained
    and crumbled
25g caster sugar
1 teaspoon orange blossom water
grated zest of 1 unwaxed lemon
¼ teaspoon table salt
40g shelled green pistachio nuts, very
    finely chopped, to decorate
35g blanched almonds, very finely
    chopped, to decorate

For the syrup
400ml dark clear honey
100ml water
grated zest and juice of ½
    unwaxed lemon
1 tablespoon orange blossom water

First make the syrup. Put the honey and water in a saucepan over a medium-high heat and stir until the honey melts. Add the lemon juice and zest and continue stirring for a minute or so, then remove from the heat and stir in the orange blossom water. Set aside until completely cool.

Preheat the oven to 200°C/Fan 180°C/Gas Mark 6 and butter the base and sides of a 30 x 30cm baking tin. You'll also need a second slightly smaller tin to press on top of the cake while it bakes.

Place the pastry in a food processor – do this in 2 or 3 goes – and blitz a few times until the strands are about 2cm long. Transfer to a bowl, pour over the melted butter and toss together so all the *kataifi* is coated. Set aside.

Put the mozzarella, ricotta, feta, sugar, orange blossom water, lemon zest and salt into a separate bowl and beat together.

Firmly press about two-thirds of the *kataifi* mixture into the base of the baking tin to compress and compact. Evenly and carefully top with the cheese mix, spreading very gently until the *kataifi* layer is covered. Finally, top with the remaining *kataifi*, pressing down firmly to cover any exposed cheese. Smooth the top and then lay a piece of baking parchment on top, followed by the second baking tin so all the ingredients are pressed down and compact.

Bake for 30 minutes, then remove the top tin and baking parchment and bake for a further 25 minutes, or until the pastry is deeply golden around the edges and browned on top.

Remove from the oven and leave on a wire rack for 10 minutes before easing a small knife around the edge to ensure it can be easily flipped out onto a chopping board or serving platter.

After you've flipped it out, drizzle a good amount of syrup over the top, then set aside for 5 minutes for the syrup to be absorbed. Sprinkle with the pistachios and almonds and serve at room temperature.

Saffron and Bay Custard Tart
with sticky blackberries

My friend Maresh is a brilliant UK-based chef originally from the Palestinian city of Rafah, and he is responsible for the conception of this recipe. It is by no means traditional, but at its heart are the flavours and spirit of Palestine. I love the striking, contrasting colours – the sticky red blackberries leaching into the vibrant yellow custard. (You can swap the blackberries for hulled strawberries in the high summer months.)

The *ma'amoul* pastry used for this tart is incredible and very easy to work with. It's a kind of Middle Eastern-style sweet biscuit, rather like a shortcrust, but nuttier thanks to the semolina flour. (For a traditional stuffed biscuit version, check out my recipe on page 205.) The pastry is traditionally flavoured with orange blossom water and ground cherry kernels (*mahlab*), both of which are available in Middle Eastern food shops and online. The custard I use here, however, is more traditional, similar to the classic Palestinian bread and custard pudding, *aish el saraya*.

Makes 6–8 slices

olive oil for greasing the tin
1 large free-range egg, beaten,
   for an egg wash

For the ma'amoul pastry
200g plain white flour
65g icing sugar
50g fine semolina flour
200g unsalted butter, chopped
1 tablespoon orange blossom water
1 teaspoon ground cherry
   kernels (*mahlab*)

For the sticky blackberries
100ml pomegranate juice
25g caster sugar
3 black peppercorns
1 cinnamon stick
grated zest of ½ unwaxed orange
200g blackberries

Preheat the oven to 200°C/Fan 180°C/Gas Mark 6. Grease a 20cm fluted tart tin with a removable base and set aside.

First make the pastry. Mix the flour, icing sugar and semolina flour together in a bowl. Melt the butter over a low heat, then pour over the flour mixture. Add the orange blossom water and ground cherry kernels and, using your fingers, mix well until you end up with a malleable pastry.

Transfer the pastry to the tart tin and use your fingers to press it across the base and up the side, leaving a good edge to account for shrinkage. Place in the fridge for 10 minutes to set.

To make the sticky blackberries, place the pomegranate juice, sugar, peppercorns, cinnamon stick and orange zest in a saucepan over a high heat and bring to a boil, then continue boiling until the liquid reduces by half. Reduce the heat to low, add the blackberries and simmer for 4 minutes, or until they are tender and the syrup is rich and sticky. Turn off the heat and set aside to cool.

Once it is cool, remove the blackberries from the syrup and set aside with the syrup separately.

Line the pastry with baking parchment and cover with baking beans or uncooked rice. Bake the pastry for 10 minutes, or until set and just baked – it should still be quite pale in colour.

For the saffron and bay custard
300ml double cream
4 fresh bay leaves
a large pinch of saffron threads
3 large free-range egg yolks and
    1 large free-range egg,
    beaten together
2 tablespoons caster sugar

Meanwhile, make the custard. Place the cream and bay leaves in a pan and heat until bubbles appear around the edge. Turn off the heat and add the saffron threads. Whisk the 3 egg yolks and the whole egg with the caster sugar in a bowl until light and pale, then slowly whisk in the warm cream until fully incorporated – do this slowly to avoid curdling. Pour back into the pan and heat very gently, stirring, until it thickens.

Remove the pan from the heat and pour the custard through a fine sieve into the pastry case, then add the bay leaves. Arrange the blackberries in the custard and finally brush the edges of the pastry with egg wash.

Place the tin on a baking sheet and return the tart to the oven for 20 minutes, or until the custard is just set and the pastry has browned. The blackberries will have started to burst through.

Place the tart on a wire rack and leave for 20 minutes before removing from the tin and leaving to cool completely. The blackberry syrup can be poured over the tart when serving.

Spiced Red Lentil Soup
with mint

This ranks among the most comforting and warming dishes I know. Lentil soups have
unfairly garnered a reputation for blandness; this vibrant Egyptian version, however, is
anything but dull – the warmly spiced, orange- and red-hued soup is popular all over
the country. The soup is usually made with a good meat or chicken stock base and
then generously spiced, before being served with yoghurt, lemon wedges and perhaps a
spoonful of dukkah stirred through at the last minute. Such is the popularity of lentil soup
in Egypt that there are specially dedicated lentil soup cafés dotted all across the country.

Serves 4

olive oil
2 onions, 1 chopped and 1 sliced
1 large carrot, peeled and
   finely chopped
2 garlic cloves, crushed
¾ teaspoon ground cumin
¾ teaspoon turmeric
¼ teaspoon red chilli powder
1.5 litres chicken stock (fresh or
   homemade is best)
150g split red lentils
juice of ½ lemon
a handful of mint leaves
sea salt and freshly ground black
   pepper

To serve
Greek yoghurt
Lemon wedges
dukkah (page 187 or shop
   bought; optional)

Heat a splash of olive oil in a saucepan over a medium heat.
When it is hot, add the chopped onion and carrot and sauté
until they are soft and just beginning to colour. Stir in the garlic,
cumin, turmeric and chilli powder, and continue stirring until
the mixture is fragrant.

Add the stock and lentils and bring to the boil, removing any
scum that appears on the surface. Reduce the heat and leave
to simmer for 30 minutes, uncovered, or until the lentils have
started to break down.

Meanwhile, heat another good splash of olive oil in a frying pan
with a tight-fitting lid over a low heat. Add the sliced onion,
cover the pan and leave to steam for 15–20 minutes until softened
but without colour. Uncover, turn up the heat to medium and
fry, stirring often, until they are dark, crisp and caramelised. Set
aside to drain on kitchen paper.

Taste and season the soup. Add some water if it needs thinning
down – it should be the consistency of double cream. Stir in the
lemon juice just before serving and garnish each bowl with the
caramelised onions and mint leaves. Serve with yoghurt, lemon
wedges and dukkah, if you like.

Aish Baladi
flatbreads flavoured with honey and allspice

These lovely flatbreads are similar to pittas, but made with wholemeal flour and traditionally baked in scorching-hot ovens in Cairo's bustling markets. They are a staple, often bought fresh twice a day, much like the French with their baguettes. Some enterprising vendors offer them as a street snack with various fillings and flavours. You should be able to achieve similar results to the clay bread ovens by using a very hot cast-iron pan placed over a hob flame.

Makes 6

7g sachet fast-action dried yeast
2 tablespoons lukewarm water
30g clear honey
1 tablespoon extra virgin olive oil,
　plus extra for greasing the bowl
1 teaspoon caster sugar
400g strong wholemeal flour
1 teaspoon ground allspice, plus extra
　for sprinkling
1 teaspoon table salt, plus extra
　for sprinkling
2 tablespoons natural yoghurt
olive oil
1 teaspoon sesame seeds

Place the yeast, water, 15g of the honey, the extra virgin olive oil and the sugar in a bowl, and mix together. Leave to stand for 5 minutes, or until the yeast begins to froth.

Place the flour, allspice and salt in a large bowl. Stir to combine and make a well in the centre. Add the yoghurt and the yeast mixture and, using your hands, mix to bring everything together to form a soft dough.

Transfer the dough to a lightly floured work surface and knead for 10–12 minutes until smooth and elastic. Place the dough in the washed, dried and greased bowl, and cover with a clean tea towel. Set aside in a warm place for 1½–2 hours until the dough has doubled in size.

Turn out the risen dough onto a lightly floured surface, then knock back and knead into a ball. Divide into 6 equal pieces. Working with one piece at a time and using floured hands, very gently press and stretch the dough to form a rough 23cm round. Repeat with the remaining dough. Cover with the tea towel until all the flatbreads are shaped.

Heat a large, cast-iron frying pan over a high heat. Working with one flatbread at a time, brush it with olive oil and dry-fry, oiled side down, for 2–3 minutes until golden and charred. Turn over and continue cooking for a further 2–3 minutes until the second side is also golden and charred. Repeat with the remaining flatbreads.

As each flatbread comes off the pan, brush it with some of the remaining honey and sprinkle with a little allspice, some sesame seeds and sea salt, then transfer to a wire rack to cool. Serve immediately as an accompaniment to a dish or with dips.

A Roasted and Stuffed Vegetable Feast
mahshi style

Egyptians love to stuff vegetables. There are meat and fish versions of the *mahshi*, but this one is completely plant based – it's a feast for the eyes and the stomach. This wonderful selection of vegetables is roasted and then filled with a delicious tomato and rice mixture laden with spices, herbs and nuts. The Egyptians call this a 'family' of vegetables, the perfect collective noun I always think. I've used tomatoes, courgettes and aubergines, but you can also use blanched chard leaves or well-rinsed vine leaves from a jar to wrap around the rice mixture. A vegetable corer is an invaluable addition to your kitchen kit to aid the stuffing process. Any vegetables left over are equally delicious the next day served cold as part of a picnic or mezze.

Serves 4–6

2 small green courgettes,
  halved widthways
2 small yellow courgettes,
  halved widthways
2 small aubergines,
  halved widthways
olive oil
leaves from a bunch of chard
2 long red Romano peppers, halved
  widthways and deseeded
2 tablespoons tomato purée
1 litre vegetable stock (fresh or
  homemade is best)
50g baby plum or cherry
  tomatoes, halved
3 fresh bay leaves

For the rice mixture
olive oil
1 small onion, finely chopped
1 teaspoon ground allspice
½ teaspoon ground cardamom
200g short-grain risotto rice
150ml vegetable stock (fresh or
  homemade is best)
30g flaked almonds
4 spring onions, thinly sliced
1 chard stalk, finely chopped
½ bunch of coriander, leaves and
  stalks chopped

First make the rice mixture. Heat a good splash of olive oil in a saucepan over a medium heat. When it is hot, add the onion and fry for a few minutes until softened but without colour. Add the allspice and cardamom and stir for 2 minutes to cook out the raw flavours, then stir in the rice, ensuring it is fully coated with the spiced oil. Season with salt and pepper, pour in the vegetable stock and bring to the boil, then simmer the rice until the liquid is nearly evaporated. Remove the pan from the heat and stir in the almonds, spring onions, chard stalk and three-quarters of the fresh herbs. The rice is still uncooked at this stage. Set aside and leave to cool.

Using a vegetable corer, teaspoon or melon baller, hollow out the courgette and aubergine halves, leaving a 0.5cm edge of flesh – you will have a sturdy cavity to fill with the rice. Set aside.

Lightly fry the aubergines in olive oil over a medium heat to blister and cook their skins. Transfer to a plate lined with kitchen paper and leave to cool.

In the same pan, over a low heat, lightly sauté the chard leaves just until they start to wilt. Transfer them to a clean tea towel and spread the leaves out fully to cool.

Now stuff the peppers, aubergines and courgettes with the rice mixture – don't overfill or pack tightly, as the rice will expand as it cooks. Lastly, divide the remaining rice mixture among the chard leaves and wrap into parcels that are fully sealed so none of the rice comes out. I use wooden cocktail sticks to keep them secure.

...ingredients and method continued on page 178

½ small bunch flat-leaf parsley,
leaves and stalks chopped
a handful of chives, chopped
fronds from a handful of
dill, chopped
sea salt and freshly ground black
pepper

Heat a generous splash of olive oil in a large flameproof casserole or sauté pan with a tight-fitting lid over a medium-high heat. When it is hot, add the tomato purée and stir for a minute or so to cook out the rawness. Place the aubergines, peppers and courgettes in the casserole, stuffed side up so as not to lose any rice. The vegetables should fit snuggly so they support each other. Drizzle with olive oil, pour around the stock and add the chopped tomatoes and bay leaves and season with salt and pepper.

Bring the liquid to the boil, then lower the heat to a simmer and add the chard parcels. Cover the casserole, reduce the heat to low and simmer for 25–30 minutes. Remove the lid and continue simmering for a further 7 minutes until all the vegetable cases are tender.

Turn off the heat and leave the vegetables to rest for 10 minutes before transferring them to a serving platter. Spoon over some of the sauce and sprinkle with the remaining fresh herbs. Serve any leftover sauce on the side.

Sesame and Anise Breadsticks

These delicious Middle Eastern breadsticks are stacked in pyramids at bakeries all across Cairo, ready for social gatherings and family feasts. Each bakery will have its own little recipe twist, perhaps in the spicing or by adding fennel seeds or saffron. Some will be dusted with icing sugar or drizzled with honey or flower water syrup. These are great as part of a mezze with good olive oil, salty sheep's cheese and perhaps some *shatta* (page 164).

Makes 12

250g strong white flour, plus
    extra for dusting
5g fresh yeast
180ml lukewarm water
1 teaspoon table salt
olive oil
50g sesame seeds
5 star anise, ground to a fine
    powder, or 1 teaspoon ground
    star anise
extra virgin olive oil for brushing

Place the flour in a large bowl and use your fingers to rub in the yeast. Make a well in the centre, add the water and salt and use your hand or a scraper to mix together until the dough forms. (You can do this in a stand mixer with the dough hook attached.) Knead for 7–8 minutes until the dough starts to become smooth, elastic and comes away easily from the side of the bowl.

Transfer the dough to a lightly floured surface and fold the sides onto the top, turn over and gently roll to create a tight ball. Transfer the dough to the washed, dried and greased bowl, cover with a tea towel and leave to rest in a warm place for 1 hour, or until it doubles in size.

Mix the sesame seeds and star anise and spread out on a baking tray. Line a baking sheet with greaseproof paper and set aside.

Turn out the dough onto a lightly floured surface, then knock back and press it into a rectangle, about 15 x 30cm and 1cm thick. Sprinkle over one quarter of the seed mix and press into the dough. Fold one-third of the dough widthways into the centre, pressing down with your fingers, sprinkle over some more seed mix and then fold the opposite third of the dough over the top. Press down again. Sprinkle with another quarter of the seed mixture and press gently into the dough. You should have a tall rectangle shape.

Using a scraper or sharp knife, cut the dough from top to bottom into twelve 1cm strips. One by one, twist each strip by pulling it the length of your baking sheet, then transfer it to the lined baking sheet, leaving a gap between each one. Cover them with a tea towel and leave to rise for 20 minutes.

Meanwhile, preheat the oven to 220°C/Fan 200°C/Gas Mark 7.

Transfer the baking sheet to the oven and mist the inside with water from a spray bottle – this gives the breadsticks an amazing, crisp finish. Bake for 8–10 minutes until golden brown. Immediately lightly brush the breadsticks with extra virgin olive oil and sprinkle over the remaining seed mix. Place on a wire rack to cool before eating.

Lamb, Sour Cherry and Pistachio Meatballs
with lemon-scented brown butter

These super-juicy lamb meatballs are packed full of flavour and texture and filled with spices, nuts and fruits. They are similar in many ways to their Sicilian and Balearic cousins, which are more usually made with pork meat.

Middle Eastern supermarkets sell two types of sour cherries – you want the less tart, sweetened ones for this recipe. (The red ones are mouth-puckering sour.)

Here I've paired the meatballs with a nutty and lemony brown butter with lots of dill, and they are delicious with rice, couscous or mashed potatoes, or simply a dollop of thick yoghurt. A good, rich tomato sauce will also work well.

Serves 4–6; makes 26 meatballs

500g minced lamb
100g shelled green pistachio nuts,
　finely chopped
2 large free-range eggs
2 garlic cloves, finely chopped
1 small onion, finely grated
2 teaspoons ground cumin
1 teaspoon ground cinnamon
a handful of sweetened sour
　cherries, pitted and chopped (see
　introduction, above)
a bunch of coriander, leaves and
　stalks finely chopped
olive oil
sea salt and freshly ground black
　pepper

For the brown butter
150g unsalted butter, chopped
1 lemon, halved
fronds of 1 bunch dill,
　roughly chopped

To make the meatballs, place the lamb, pistachios, eggs, garlic, onion, ground cumin and cinnamon, sour cherries and fresh coriander in a bowl. Season well with salt and pepper and use your hands to mix together until fully combined. Divide the mix into 26 equal portions and roll into balls the size of ping-pong balls. Place them on a tray and transfer to the fridge for at least 20 minutes or up to 24 hours.

Heat a good splash of olive oil in a large sauté pan over a medium-low heat. When it is hot, add as many meatballs as will fit without overcrowding the pan. Fry for 12 minutes or so until they are nicely browned with a crust all over and the juices run clear when you cut one open. Set aside and keep warm if you have to cook in batches.

When all the meatballs have been cooked, add the butter to the pan and use a wooden spoon to scrape the base to transfer any sediment into the butter. When the butter starts to foam and turns a nutty brown, squeeze in the lemon juice. Remove the pan from the heat, stir in the dill and season.

Baste all the meatballs with the butter sauce and then serve.

Filo and Coconut Custard
with dried fruits

Many cultures have a version of bread-and-butter pudding, an essential, frugal and delicious way to use up old and stale bread or pastry. *Om Ali*, translated as 'Mother of Ali', was created after the ending of a long-fought civil war with the instruction that it was to be made and present on all the Egyptian tables, thus becoming the nation's culinary signal of peace. The eggs and bread in most recipes are replaced here by shards of crisp filo or puff pastry, and though still very rich this has a lightness not usually associated with bread-and-butter puddings.

There are many variations of this dish, but the basic principles remain the same – layered pastry is filled with butter and sweet cream and then baked. My version includes nuts, dried fruit and desiccated coconut, but you can grate in dark chocolate, sprinkle over pomegranate seeds or fold fresh mint leaves and citrus zest through the cream.

Serves 6–8

100g filo pastry
50g unsalted butter, melted, plus
   extra for buttering the baking tin
50g sultanas
50g semi-dried apricots
40g flaked almonds
25g chopped shelled pistachio nuts
25 g chopped pine nuts
25g desiccated coconut
400ml whole milk
250ml clotted cream
60g golden caster sugar
1 teaspoon ground cinnamon

Preheat the oven to 220°C/Fan 200°C/Gas Mark 7.

First bake the filo pastry. Arrange the pastry sheets in a single layer on a large baking sheet and brush with the melted butter, scrunching the pastry a little. Transfer to the oven and bake for 8 minutes, or until all the pastry is crisp and golden brown. Carefully transfer the pastry sheets to a wire rack and leave to cool. Do this in batches if necessary.

Meanwhile, butter a 23–25cm baking dish or pie dish and set aside. Mix the sultanas, apricots, almonds, pistachios, pine nuts and coconut together, and set aside.

Roughly break up one-third of the filo sheets and drop them into the buttered dish – you just want the shards to cover the base. Sprinkle over half of the nuts, coconut and dried fruit, then top with another layer of broken-up filo, followed by the rest of the nuts, coconut and fruit, and a final layer of filo. Transfer the dish into a baking tray.

Put the milk, clotted cream and sugar in a saucepan, and bring to a simmer, stirring to dissolve the sugar. Pour this over the layered pie dish. Sprinkle over some of the cinnamon, then transfer to the oven. Bake for 15 minutes, or until the cream is bubbling and thickened and the top has turned golden brown.

Leave to stand for 10 minutes before serving, sprinkled with the remaining ground cinnamon.

Pistachio and Sea Salt Caramel

Egyptians have a very sweet tooth. This delicious set, nutty caramel, not unlike
a brittle, is a street food snack that is ideal served alongside strong coffee. The salt
adds a contrasting edge to the teeth-jangling sweet caramel. I like to serve this at the
end of a meal, broken into rustic shards and extravagantly piled onto a serving plate.
You can also break it into smaller shards and use it to decorate cakes and desserts.

Serves 4

100g caster sugar
1 teaspoon sea salt
2 tablespoons cold water
50g shelled pistachio nuts

Line a large baking sheet with baking parchment and set aside.

Put the sugar and salt in a small saucepan over a low heat. Add
the water and give the pan a few gentle shakes to help the sugar
dissolve into the water. Once the sugar has dissolved, increase
the heat a little and bring the syrup to a gentle simmer. Keep
simmering for about 8 minutes until the syrup turns a deep
golden colour – it should resemble golden syrup.

Add the pistachios to the caramel and give the pan a gentle shake
to incorporate. Pour onto the baking parchment, flatten out with
the back of a large wet spoon and leave to completely cool and
become firm. Break into shards and serve with strong hot coffee.
It will keep for up to a week in an airtight container.

Dukkah

Dukkah is an essential spice-and-nut mix condiment that is as delicious as it is versatile, bursting with complex flavours with a crunchy texture. I always keep a jar to hand to sprinkle over anything from salads and eggs to grilled fish or roasted meat. It is also excellent when stirred into slow-cooked dishes at the end of the cooking time to add a vibrant flavour boost and help thicken the sauce.

Sometimes I add fresh herbs to my dukkah, especially if planning to make it as a dressing, but this is a traditional version.

Makes about 200g

50g sesame seeds
25g coriander seeds
2 teaspoons black onion (nigella) seeds
1 teaspoon cumin seeds
½ teaspoon dried chilli flakes
3 tablespoons extra virgin olive oil
juice of ½ lemon
50g blanched hazelnuts, chopped
50g shelled pistachio nuts, chopped
a handful of dill fronds or parsley
   leaves, finely chopped (optional)
sea salt and freshly ground black
   pepper

Place the sesame, coriander, nigella and cumin seeds and chilli flakes in a pestle and mortar, and crush for a few minutes to break up. Transfer them to a bowl and add the extra virgin olive oil and lemon juice. Add the hazelnuts and pistachios and season with salt and pepper.

Set aside and leave for an hour or so at room temperature for the flavours to develop. Stir in a handful of fresh herbs, if you wish, just before serving. It will keep for up to 2 months in an airtight jar in the fridge or somewhere else cool.

southern shores

Tunisia
Algeria
Morocco

The southern shores of the Mediterranean, where the sea kisses the Maghreb region of North Africa, has a charm all of its own. A world where Berber, Arab and French influences feed into an intriguing and vibrant food culture that has given this shoreline of the mighty Mediterranean its particular and singular cuisine.

Over the centuries, the countries that sit on the southern shores have absorbed an influx of competing and intoxicating food traditions.

The Middle East and Muslim world brought a tradition of heavy spicing, the use of fresh herbs, dried fruits and nuts, chilli heat and grilling over hot charcoal. The French brought their love of sweet things – fried almond pastries, date shortbreads, classic crème caramels and choux pastries are to be found all over the region, gently scented with local aromatic flower waters or studded with dried fruits. It is a sun-blessed world of heady flavours and intermingled culinary delights. Here are a few of my favourite things to be found on the southern shores.

Tagines and tangias

Shape, scents, construct, tradition and practicalities – the tagine is culinary form and function at its best. Long, slow cooking in a tagine, the conical shaped cooking pot of North Africa, is a staple of the region. Cooking in a tagine is a technique that yields incredibly tender dishes and also manages to harness and deliver intense flavours.

Delicious preparations are to be found everywhere – from bustling street vendor stalls to the grandest and most famed of landmark restaurants. I adore the tagine, both as a favoured kitchen utensil and also for the dishes that are cooked within. It is one of my favourite workhorse kitchen pots. I especially love the theatricality of the big reveal as the lid is removed and the sensuous hit of cooking aromas wafts across and around the table.

And then there are the tangias. Most often served as a meat preparation packed with spices, fruits and a little broth, all bundled into a clay pot, sealed and then cooked overnight in the dying embers of a fire. Though originally designed to cook and tenderise the toughest of meats, the tangia is also a perfect vessel to harness and develop depth of flavour. In Algeria, the tangia is often topped with a spice-crusted pastry lid made from semolina flour and ghee, rather like a pastry pie top, with a little steam hole in the centre.

These wonderful slow-cooked meals are usually served with steaming bowls of couscous doused in olive oil and accompanied with a bowl of homemade harissa on the side.

Harissa

Ah, harissa. One of my very favourite things. The North Africans' addiction to spice and heat is legendary, and with harissa they have the perfect condiment to carry the love. As popular as ketchup is in the West, harissa sits proudly on the table at breakfast, lunch and dinner. Though widely available in local shops, it is often made at home to a specific and treasured family recipe, like my version on page 200.

Moroccan harissa is made from red chillies, while in Tunisia you'll find it made with green chillies. The best harissa uses chillies that have been grilled over fire for a wonderful smoky flavour.

Preserved lemons

Salty and sour with umami complexity and infinite possibilities, the preserved lemon is a vibrant creation of wonder and singularity. The rinds are delicious chopped into salads or bowls of couscous, or deep-fried to serve alongside squid to give astringency and edge. The whole fruit becomes a wonderful seasoning when added to stews and casseroles. When used in deeply sweet desserts they act as a perfect counterpoint to give balance. With rich creamy cheeses they become the ideal partner. Was ever something so unexpected quite so extraordinarily versatile?

The street food markets and souks

The whirlwind experience of diving into the souks and street food markets of North Africa is a heady existential experience and not for the faint hearted – sounds, sights, smells, chatter, barter and banter. It's a glorious affirmation of life and a rude shock to the sensibilities of the more circumspect Western visitor. But once experienced, never forgotten and soon mastered.

The Jemaa el-Fnaa, located in the central square in Marrakesh's old city, is one such market. Scores of food stalls encircle and fill the square, each specialising in a specific food or preparation. Simply arrive, make your choice and eat stallside. Everything from vegetable preparations, meat stews, spiced food in bread wraps, North African sweets, fried eggs or lamb intestines with harissa, and even chewy snail kebabs, lined up in pyramid stacks ready to be cooked over a hot grill.

Eating like a local

The joy of eating like a local is part of the essential experience of visiting any foreign country – and nowhere more so than North Africa.

In Marrakesh, there is a famed local restaurant called Le Tobsil, on the back streets of the Medina behind an unassuming ornate wooden door with a tiny brass sign reading 'Tobsil'. This is the sole indication of what delights lie inside this grand riad, housed within a typical Moroccan Tardis-like dining room. The food is served family style. To begin, some warm Moroccan flatbreads with tiny saucers of salads and condiments – harissa, candied vegetables, roasted aubergines, grilled peppers, chopped raw lamb, saffron-infused yoghurts and much more. All exquisite.

Next a tagine of chicken followed by a tagine of lamb, both highly flavoured and meltingly tender. A couple of decadent desserts to finish – perhaps crème brûlée with pomegranate seeds and rose petals and maybe a pear poached with spices and bitter orange juice and rind. To finish, silver pots of steaming fresh mint tea and an intoxicating, tassel-spinning performance from a traditional musician and entertainer. This is how to eat, very well, like a local.

Cumin-roasted Aubergines and Blood Orange
with a pomegranate-flavoured dressing and mint

I first came across this wonderful roasted vegetable and orange mash-up at a beach picnic in Tunisia. A rickety stall just off the side of the beach was selling a variety of stuffed flatbreads known as *malfouf*. Tuna with lemon and sliced omelette, fried potatoes and harissa was one, and this one was the other, in which all the ingredients had been left to marinade in the oily juices, with mint leaves added at the end.

These tomatoes and aubergines are excellent wrapped in flatbreads, perfect on their own or as an accompaniment to grilled and barbecued meats.

Serves 4

2 plum vine tomatoes, halved
   widthways
16 cherry vine tomatoes, halved
   widthways
1 small blood orange or plain orange,
   thinly sliced
olive oil
1 aubergine, ends trimmed and cut
   into 8–10 wedges
1 teaspoon cumin seeds,
   lightly crushed
a large handful of fresh mint leaves
a pinch of Aleppo pepper or dried
   red chilli flakes
sea salt and freshly ground black
   pepper

For the dressing
40ml extra virgin olive oil, plus
   extra for drizzling
2 teaspoons pomegranate molasses
2 teaspoons red wine vinegar
seeds from ½ pomegranate

Preheat the oven to 180°C/Fan 160°C/Gas Mark 4.

Place the tomatoes, cut side up, and the orange slices in a roasting tin and season. Drizzle with olive oil and roast for 20–30 minutes until caramelised and the juices are bubbling. You will need to monitor and remove each ingredient when it is ready – the cherry tomatoes will be ready first, then the oranges and finally the larger tomatoes.

In a separate tin, douse the aubergine pieces in olive oil, season and sprinkle with the cumin. Add them to the oven and roast for about 30 minutes until they are tender and golden brown. Set aside.

To make the dressing, whisk the extra virgin olive oil with the pomegranate molasses, vinegar and the pomegranate seeds. Season lightly.

Assemble all the roasted fruit – yes, tomatoes are botanically a fruit – and aubergine wedges on a serving plate or in a bowl. While they are still lukewarm, spoon over the dressing. Cover and set aside at room temperature for an hour or so.

To serve, sprinkle over the mint leaves and Aleppo pepper and drizzle with olive oil.

Kerkennah-style Grilled Prawns

On the Kerkennah islands just off the coast of Tunisia, seafood is often paired with kerkennaise, a spiced tomato sauce with subtle chilli heat, pungent spicing and lots of spring onions, olives and capers. It is a sublime mix of Moorish and Mediterranean flavours. Use this sauce for any grilled fish, squid or octopus.

Serves 4; the sauce makes about 200ml

16 large Atlantic prawns, heads
   removed and the tail shells
   peeled off
olive oil
sea salt and freshly ground black
   pepper

For the sauce
10 spring onions, white parts chopped
   and green ends thinly sliced
2 plum vine tomatoes, cut into
   large chunks
1 large green chilli, trimmed,
   quartered lengthways and deseeded
1 garlic clove, crushed
½ teaspoon ground coriander
½ teaspoon caraway seeds,
   lightly ground
½ teaspoon cumin seeds,
   lightly ground
2 tablespoons red wine vinegar,
   such as cabernet sauvignon
a handful of pitted green
   olives, chopped
a handful of flat-leaf parsley leaves,
   roughly chopped
1 tablespoon tomato purée
extra virgin olive oil

First make the sauce. Blitz the spring onion whites, tomatoes, green chilli, garlic, ground coriander, caraway and cumin seeds and vinegar together in a blender. Transfer this mixture to a bowl, stir in the spring onion greens, olives, parsley, tomato purée and a good splash of extra virgin olive oil. Cover the bowl with cling film and let it rest while you heat the barbecue.

Light the barbecue about 30 minutes before you want to cook so the coals turn ashen grey and are at the optimum grilling temperature. Position the grill above the coals so it gets very hot. Alternatively, heat a large ridged, cast-iron griddle pan to maximum.

When you're ready to grill, pat the prawns dry, then rub them with a little olive oil and season with salt and pepper. Place on the grill and grill for 3 minutes on each side until the prawns change colour and are cooked through – a little charring adds a smoky flavour.

Transfer the prawns to a serving platter or individual plates and spoon over some of the sauce. Serve the remaining sauce on the side for everyone to help themselves.

My Harissa

Harissa is an ever-present and reassuring North African culinary phenomenon. There are countless variations to be discovered, varying in heat and spice defined by region and tradition.

One rule, though, is sacrosanct – the chilli peppers must be grilled over fire, either on a barbecue or over the flame of a gas hob. Once blistered and the smoky heat of the chilli is released, the alchemy of spice and olive oil plays its magical part and the harissa is created.

Makes 150–200g

24 fresh red chillies
2 teaspoons coriander seeds
1 teaspoon caraway seeds
1 teaspoon cumin seeds
7 garlic cloves, roughly chopped
2 teaspoons sea salt flakes
5 tablespoons light extra virgin
   olive oil
1 tablespoon tomato purée
4 teaspoons lemon juice

Light a barbecue before you want to cook so the coals turn ashen grey and it is at medium heat. Position the grill above the coals.

Add the chillies and grill for 20 minutes, turning them, until the skins blacken and the flesh is tender. If you don't have a barbecue, hold the chillies with heatproof tongs over a gas flame and carefully blacken the skins, then transfer to a baking tray and roast at 200°C/Fan 180°C/Gas Mark 6 for 15–20 minutes until tender.

Transfer the chillies to a plastic bag or a bowl covered with cling film and leave to steam and cool. When cool enough to handle, remove the stalks and peel the chillies. Split them lengthways, scrape out the seeds with a knife and discard. Don't rinse the chillies or you'll lose the smoky flavour. Set aside.

Toast the coriander, caraway and cumin seeds in a dry frying pan over a medium heat until they are fragrant, stirring so they don't burn. Use a pestle and mortar or spice grinder to make a fine powder. Add the chillies, garlic and sea salt flakes, then grind to a fine paste. Stir in the extra virgin olive oil, tomato purée and lemon juice, then set aside for at least 3 hours for the flavours to develop before using.

Honey and Harissa Chicken Wings
with preserved lemon marmalade and fresh herbs

This is such a delicious dish, with the smoky grilled hot-and-sweet chicken wings offset by the slightly sour preserved lemons; it is typical of the full-flavoured mezzes and grills of Tunisia. Accompany with breads and dips.

Serves 4

12 chicken wings
a small handful each of dill fronds
    and basil, coriander and flat-leaf
    parsley leaves, to serve

For the preserved lemon marmalade
100ml water
4 preserved lemons, quartered,
    flesh and pith removed and the
    rinds cut into strips
2 tablespoons orange marmalade
2 tablespoons caster sugar

For the marinade
100ml extra virgin olive oil, plus
    extra for the herb salad
75ml runny honey
2 garlic cloves, sliced
1 tablespoon harissa (page 200
    or shop bought)
juice of 1 lemon
1 teaspoon cumin seeds
1 teaspoon table salt

Light a barbecue about 30 minutes before you want to cook so the coals turn ashen grey and are at the optimum grilling temperature. Position the grill above the coals so it gets very hot. Alternatively, heat a large ridged, cast-iron griddle pan to maximum.

First make the marmalade. Place the water, preserved lemon rinds, orange marmalade and sugar in a small saucepan over a high heat and bring to the boil, stirring to dissolve the sugar. Reduce heat to medium-low and simmer for 8–10 minutes, frequently brushing down the sides of the pan, until you have a jammy consistency. Remove from the heat and leave to cool.

To make the marinade, mix the extra virgin olive oil, honey, garlic, harissa, lemon juice, cumin seeds and table salt in a large non-metallic bowl. Add the chicken wings, coating each with the marinade, then leave them in the fridge for 25 minutes.

Lift the chicken wings out of the marinade, letting the excess drip back into the bowl. Place them on the grill, meatier side down, and grill for 10 minutes, then turn and cook for a further 5 minutes, or until caramelised and the juices run clear.

Meanwhile, toss the herbs with a splash of extra virgin olive oil in a bowl. Place the chicken on a plate, scatter over the herbs and serve with the marmalade on the side.

Lamb Kofte
with Nykeeta's lime-pickled red onions

I give you the perfect kofte. I was given the recipe by a friend who lives in Tunis and it's a cracker. The minced lamb must be left well alone after the pine nuts and other flavourings are added to allow the spices to infuse and develop. Cook over a barbecue on skewers or under a kitchen grill. Serve with warmed pitta breads (page 154 or shop bought), Greek yoghurt and the dazzling pickled red onions perfected by my wife, Nykeeta. A tomato salad is a good accompaniment, too.

Makes 8

2 small onions, grated
a small bunch of mint leaves, chopped
a small bunch of flat-leaf
    parsley, chopped
750g minced lamb
50g dried breadcrumbs
50g pine nuts, toasted and chopped
2 garlic cloves, finely grated
1½ teaspoons ground allspice
1½ teaspoons ground fenugreek
1½ teaspoons ground nutmeg
1½ teaspoons freshly ground black
    pepper
1 teaspoon sea salt
olive oil
1 tablespoon pomegranate molasses
    for glazing
pitta breads (page 154 or shop
    bought), warmed, to serve
Greek yoghurt, to serve

For Nykeeta's lime-pickled onions
2 small red onions, halved and
    thinly sliced
2 teaspoons caster sugar
pinch of salt
juice and grated zest of 2
    unwaxed limes

To make the kofte mixture, use your hands to squeeze any moisture from the grated onions, then mix them with the mint and parsley in a large bowl. Add the lamb, breadcrumbs, pine nuts, garlic and ground allspice, fenugreek, nutmeg, pepper and the salt, and mix together until fully combined. Shape into 8 kofte 'fingers', then cover with cling film and chill for at least 2 hours or up to 12 hours.

For the pickled onions, place the onion slices into a non-metallic bowl, sprinkle over the sugar and a pinch of salt, and toss together. Add the lime juice and zest, then set aside for at least an hour before using – the onion slices will turn a day-glo pink.

Light a barbecue about 30 minutes before you want to cook so the coals turn ashen grey and are at the optimum grilling temperature. Position the grill above the coals so it gets very hot. Alternatively, heat a large ridged, cast-iron griddle pan to maximum.

Rub the koftes with olive oil. Place them on the grill and grill for 8–9 minutes until golden brown all round and until just pink in the centre – if you want them well done, keep grilling for a further 2–4 minutes.

Transfer the koftas to a platter and brush them with the molasses. Serve immediately with the pickled onions, pitta breads and Greek yoghurt.

Clementine and Pomegranate Cake

This was inspired by food writer Claudia Roden's recipe for her whole orange and almond cake in her *A Book of Middle Eastern Food* from 1968. The recipe is still as exciting and fresh as ever. Here's my homage to it.

Serves 6–8

4 clementines or satsumas, unpeeled
1 cinnamon stick
olive oil for greasing the tin
6 large free-range eggs
225g light muscovado sugar
300g ground almonds
1 teaspoon baking powder
icing sugar for dusting

For the syrup
1 pomegranate, halved
25g light muscovado sugar
1 teaspoon orange blossom water
1 teaspoon vanilla bean paste

For the apricot glaze
3 tablespoons apricot jam

Place the clementines and cinnamon stick in a medium saucepan over a high heat with enough cold water to cover and bring to the boil. Reduce the heat to very low, cover the pan and leave to simmer for 1 hour. Drain the fruit and discard the cinnamon stick. Leave to cool for 30 minutes, then halve the cooked fruit and discard the pips. Put the fruit, including the peel, into a blender or food processor and blend to a purée. Set aside.

Preheat the oven to 200°C/Fan 180°C/Gas Mark 6. Grease and line a 23cm cake tin that is 9cm deep.

Using an electric hand whisk, whisk the eggs and sugar in a heatproof bowl over a saucepan of barely simmering water for about 5 minutes until pale and mousse-like. Take the bowl off the heat and add the ground almonds, baking powder and the fruit purée. Fold in gently, but thoroughly. Spoon the batter into the cake tin and smooth the surface. Bake for 20 minutes, then reduce the oven temperature to 180°C/Fan 160°C/Gas Mark 4 and continue baking for a further 30 minutes, or until a skewer inserted into the centre comes out clean. Leave to cool slightly in the tin for 15 minutes.

Meanwhile, make the syrup. Squeeze the pomegranate halves to extract the juice over a small saucepan and set aside the seeds. Add the sugar to the juice, stirring to dissolve, and bring to the boil, then simmer for 2 minutes. Leave to cool slightly, then stir in the orange blossom water and vanilla paste.

While the cake and syrup are both still warm, use a pastry brush to brush syrup over the cake. Leave the cake in the tin until it is completely cold.

To make the apricot glaze, put the jam into a small saucepan and gently warm through, then pass through a sieve.

Remove the cool cake from the tin and place on a serving plate. If the cake has sunk a little in the middle, you can turn it upside-down for a flat and even finish. Using a pastry brush, brush the apricot glaze all over the cake. Just before serving, scatter the reserved pomegranate seeds over the top of the cake and dust with icing sugar.

Ma'amouls
date shortbreads

A popular Tunisian butter-laden biscuit stuffed with a sticky-sweet date paste, these are very rich and incredibly delicious. Traditionally these biscuits are made by pressing the raw paste into lightly floured, especially designed decorative *ma'amoul* moulds that are readily available online, but you can also shape them using your hands. The ground cherry kernels (*mahlab*) add a distinctive bittersweet note, and you can buy them in Middle Eastern food shops or online.

Makes 12

185g fine semolina flour, plus extra
    for dusting
30g plain white flour
25g caster sugar
½ teaspoon ground cherry
    kernels (*mahlab*)
90g unsalted butter, diced
2 teaspoons orange blossom water
2 teaspoons rosewater
1 egg yolk, beaten with a splash of
    milk, for an egg wash
icing sugar for dusting

For the filling
150g Medjool dates, pitted
    and chopped
2 tablespoons rosewater
1 teaspoon ground cinnamon
1 teaspoon ground cherry
    kernels (*mahlab*)

Mix the semolina flour, white flour, sugar and ground cherry kernels together in a bowl. Use your fingertips to rub in the butter until the mixture resembles fine crumbs. Add the orange blossom and rose waters and bring the dough together with your hands. Tip the dough out onto a work surface lightly dusted with semolina flour and knead for a few minutes until it is smooth. Roll into a ball, wrap in cling film and chill for 30 minutes to rest.

Meanwhile, preheat the oven to 200°C/Fan 180°C/Gas Mark 6. Line a baking sheet with baking parchment and set aside.

To make the date filling, place the dates in a blender with the rosewater, ground cinnamon and ground cherry kernels, and blitz to a smooth paste. Divide the mixture into 12 equal portions and roll into balls. Cover and leave to rest for 5 minutes.

Divide the dough into 12 equal portions and roll into balls. One at a time, lightly press each ball against a lightly dusted work surface to flatten, then push your thumb gently into the centre to make a cavity. Add a ball of filling, then ease the dough over the top and pinch to seal. Roll into a smooth ball, then flatten slightly again on the work surface and transfer to the baking sheet. If you are using a *ma'amoul* mould, lightly dust it with semolina flour and tip out the excess. Add one stuffed dough ball and press the mould together. Tip out the shaped biscuit and transfer to the baking sheet. Repeat until all the biscuits are shaped. Brush the biscuits with the egg wash before baking.

Transfer the baking sheet to the oven and bake the biscuits for about 15 minutes until golden brown on the bottom and lightly golden on top. Remove from the oven and transfer to a wire rack to cool completely. Dust with icing sugar just before serving.

Muhammara
grilled red pepper and walnut dip

Muhammara is a delicious and versatile Algerian paste. You can use it as a dip for pitta breads, spooned over grilled vegetables, as an accompaniment for grilled fish and meat or stirred into stews to add a smoky-sweet depth of flavour. It can be made in larger batches and stored in the fridge in a covered airtight container for up to a month.

Makes about 200ml

8 red peppers
olive oil
3 tablespoons extra virgin olive oil,
   plus extra to serve
70g walnut halves, plus extra,
   to garnish
½ teaspoon cumin seeds, toasted in
   a dry pan until fragrant and then
   ground to a powder
2 tablespoons Turkish hot pepper
   paste (*biber salcasi*), or 2 fresh
   red chillies, deseeded and
   finely chopped
50g dry white breadcrumbs
3 tablespoons pomegranate molasses
1 garlic clove
sea salt and freshly ground black
   pepper

Light a barbecue about 30 minutes before you want to cook so the coals turn ashen grey and are at the optimum grilling temperature. Position the grill above the coals so it gets very hot. Alternatively, heat a large ridged, cast-iron griddle pan to maximum.

Rub the peppers with olive oil and grill them over the coals, turning occasionally, until completely charred and blackened. Transfer them to a bowl, cover with cling film and leave for 10 minutes to steam – this makes it easier to peel off the skins.

When the peppers are cool enough to handle, cut them in half and remove the cores and skins.

Place all the ingredients in a blender and blitz to a paste. Season to taste. Cover and chill until required. Garnish with a few extra walnut halves and a drizzle of oil before serving.

Pilav
with spring vegetables and herbs

North African *pilavs* are a personal favourite – the rice is steamed in a pot with a good stock to make a light and aromatic dish with just the right amount of flavour and moisture. It's a dish borne out of poverty and frugality from a desire to maximise flavour with very little to hand. This dish is delicious on its own with just the simple addition of labneh or *Muhammara* (page 208).

Serves 4

75g unsalted butter
6 allspice berries
1 cinnamon stick
1 large onion, thinly sliced
300g basmati rice, soaked in
   lukewarm water for 1 hour
4 cooked baby artichoke hearts in
   brine, drained and quartered
1 bunch of spring onions, quartered
   lengthways
120g frozen broad beans, defrosted
   and removed from the grey 'jackets'
80g fresh or frozen shelled peas
450ml vegetable or chicken stock
   (fresh or homemade is best)
1 bunch of asparagus, woody ends
   trimmed, stalks sliced and tips
   kept intact
3 fresh bay leaves
fronds from 1 bunch of dill, chopped
a handful of mint leaves, chopped
juice of ½ lemon
sea salt and freshly ground black
   pepper

Melt the butter in a large saucepan with a tight-fitting lid over a medium heat. Add the allspice and cinnamon stick and stir until the butter foams. Add the onion, lower the heat and cook slowly, stirring occasionally, for 20 minutes to soften and brown.

Meanwhile, drain the rice and set aside.

Add the artichokes and spring onions to the pan and cook for 1 minute. Add the rice, stirring to coat it in the butter for a minute or so. Now add the broad beans, peas, stock, asparagus, bay leaves and half the dill. Season well, cover with greaseproof paper and then the lid.

Bring to the boil, then turn the heat down to medium-low and simmer for 5 minutes before turning the heat to very low for a final 5 minutes. Turn off the heat and leave the *pilav* to rest for 5 minutes before removing the lid and parchment.

Give everything a good stir, then stir in the mint, lemon juice and remaining dill. Serve.

Potato Salad
with harissa and caraway seeds

Here's a vibrant potato salad that is both sharp and sweet and so typical of the highly flavoured herby dishes of North Africa. It's delicious on its own or as a side served with grilled chicken or lamb – I like to leave the grilled meat to rest over the salad so the meaty juices soak into the potatoes and mix in with the vinegar and oil. I use pink fir or ratte potatoes for this, but new potatoes are just fine, too.

Serves 4

750g small waxy potatoes, peeled and halved
2 garlic cloves, finely chopped
1 red onion, finely chopped
leaves from a small bunch of flat-leaf parsley, finely chopped
2 tablespoons sweet white wine vinegar, such as muscatel or chardonnay
2 teaspoons harissa (page 200 or shop bought), plus extra to serve
2 heaped teaspoons caraway seeds, lightly toasted
extra virgin olive oil
labneh or Greek yoghurt, to serve
sea salt and freshly ground black pepper

Place the potatoes in a saucepan with enough salted water to cover. Bring to the boil, then boil until they are tender – the tip of a knife should slide in easily. Drain well and leave to cool until they can be peeled by hand.

Put the peeled potatoes in a large bowl. Add the garlic, red onion, parsley, vinegar, harissa and caraway seeds. Season well and add 2 good splashes of extra virgin olive oil. Mix well, cover and leave for 20 minutes before serving.

Serve on labneh or yoghurt with extra harissa to be spooned over and mixed in to taste.

Spiced Fried Chicken
with sultanas and pine nuts

I will never forget the amazing sight and aromas of this wonderful dish as it was being prepared kerb-side in one of Algeria's bustling food markets. A large vat of olive oil bubbled away as chicken pieces were cooked to golden and then scooped out to be topped with a citrus-and-spiced-infused sauce. It was served with a flatbread to scoop up all the deliciousness. Street food doesn't get much better.

My version has been translated into a one-pan dish with the chicken sitting in a delicious sultana and pine nut sauce. This is a firm Tish family favourite served with the potato salad on page 210.

Serves 4

8 boneless chicken thighs
40g plain white flour
olive oil
a handful of mint leaves, to serve
a handful of flat-leaf parsley leaves,
    chopped, to serve
sea salt and freshly ground black
    pepper

For the marinade
4 garlic cloves, finely chopped
2 fresh red chillies, deseeded and
    finely chopped
4 tablespoons pine nuts
4 tablespoons sultanas
2 teaspoons crushed dried chilli flakes
2 teaspoons ground cinnamon
2 teaspoons ground cumin
1 tablespoon extra virgin olive oil
juice of 1 lemon
juice of 1 orange

Place the chicken pieces in a shallow dish. Mix all the marinade ingredients together, then pour over the chicken. Leave to marinate for about 1 hour in the fridge.

Remove the chicken from the marinade, wiping off any excess. Dredge each piece in the flour, then season well and set aside. Do not discard the marinade.

Heat a good 2cm olive oil in a large sauté pan over a medium heat. When it is hot, add the chicken pieces and shallow-fry until golden brown. Turn them over and continue frying a further 2–3 minutes until the other side is golden brown. You will probably have to do this in batches, so remove the chicken thighs as they are cooked, and top up the oil as required.

Remove the pan from the heat and carefully pour the excess oil into a bowl. Place the pan over a high heat, pour in the reserved marinade and boil it for 2–3 minutes. Reduce the heat, return the chicken pieces to the pan, season with salt and pepper and simmer for 2–3 minutes until all the pieces are fully cooked through.

Scatter over the mint and parsley and serve.

Spicy Beef Hariri

Heart-warming, robust and tasty, *hariri* is usually made with lamb, but my beef version is a less-fatty alternative. Closer to a soup than a stew, the beef is a team player here with the lentils and chickpeas playing equal parts to help mollify the hot tomato sauce, aromatic spices and cooking juices.

Serves 4

olive oil
600g boneless beef chuck, diced
3 garlic cloves, finely chopped
1 onion, finely chopped
1 tablespoon tomato purée
3 fresh bay leaves
2 teaspoons *ras el hanout*
1 teaspoon chilli powder
1 teaspoon coriander seeds, crushed
½ teaspoon ground cloves
700ml beef stock (fresh or
    homemade is best)
400g tinned chopped tomatoes
leaves from 1 bunch of
    coriander, chopped
100g dried green lentils
400g tinned chickpeas, drained
    and rinsed
juice of ½ lemon
sea salt and freshly ground black
    pepper

To serve
2 eggs
1 bunch of spring onions, thinly sliced
pitta breads (page 154 or shop bought)
Greek yoghurt
harissa (page 200 or shop bought)

Heat a good splash of olive oil in a large saucepan over medium-high heat. Season the beef, and fry in batches for 4–5 minutes until caramelised. Remove from the pan and set aside.

Add the garlic and onion to the oil remaining in the pan and fry, stirring, for 3–4 minutes until softened. Add the tomato purée, bay leaves, *ras el hanout*, chilli powder, coriander seeds and ground cloves, and stir for 2 minutes. Stir in the beef so it is well coated. Add the stock, chopped tomatoes and three-quarters of the fresh coriander, and bring to a simmer. Cover the pan, reduce the heat to low and leave to simmer for 1 hour.

Meanwhile, rinse the lentils and leave them to soak in water to cover for 20 minutes.

Drain the lentils and stir them into the pan along with the chickpeas. Re-cover the pan and continue simmering for a further 30 minutes.

To soft-boil the eggs for serving, bring a pan of water to the boil. Gently lower in the eggs and let them simmer for 7 minutes. Drain them in a sieve, then run cold running water over them to stop the cooking. When they are cool enough to handle, shell them and set aside.

Remove the lid from the saucepan, give everything a good stir and continue simmering over a low heat for a further 30 minutes, or until the beef is super tender and the soup is slightly reduced and thickened. Season to taste and stir in the lemon juice.

Divide among bowls and finish each with the spring onions and remaining coriander leaves. Cut the eggs in half and nestle them in the soup. This is delicious served with pitta breads, yoghurt and a dollop of harissa.

Cardamom-scented Custard
with strawberries

This recipe was inspired by a very simple dessert I first had at an Algerian restaurant –
basically a set cream with fresh raspberries and cardamom thickened with ground rice.
The soft summer fruits and berries have a natural affinity with the cardamom.

My version is a little lighter and creamier and I add some rosewater, which goes elegantly
with the strawberries. Make in individual ramekins or in one large bowl, trifle style, for
the table.

Serves 6

400ml double cream
300ml whole milk
1 tablespoon cardamom seeds
6 large free-range egg yolks
75g caster sugar
1 tablespoon cornflour
1 teaspoon rosewater
200g fresh strawberries, hulled
    and halved or quartered
    depending on size
juice of ½ lemon
30g dark brown soft sugar
a handful of unsprayed pink rose
    petals (optional)

Heat the cream, milk and cardamom seeds in a heavy-based
saucepan over a low heat, stirring occasionally, for 20 minutes,
or until the mixture just starts to boil. Strain through a fine sieve
into a jug and discard the seeds.

Whisk the egg yolks, sugar and cornflour in a bowl (or use a
stand mixer) until light and airy. Add the cream mixture and
continue whisking until well incorporated.

To finish the custard, pour the mixture into a saucepan over a
medium-low heat. Add the rosewater and stir constantly with a
wooden spoon for 15 minutes, or until the custard thickens and
coats the back of the spoon.

Strain the custard through the sieve into a serving bowl or
individual bowls and leave to cool, then cover the surface with
cling film and chill for at least an hour or up to 24 hours. The
custard will set.

Meanwhile, 20 minutes before serving, toss the strawberries in
the lemon juice and sugar and leave to macerate.

To serve, spoon over the strawberries and any liquid that's left
from macerating over the custard. A sprinkle of rose petals is
nice, if you like.

Lacy Pancakes
with roasted stone fruit, labneh and lavender

The Maghrebi *baghrirs* are delicious, light and lacy pancakes eaten all over North Africa and Turkey, enjoyed from breakfast to dinnertime. The yeast and baking powder in the batter cause it to bubble and rise immediately on cooking to form '1000' holes ready to catch any and all the flavours on offer. I like to serve these with roasted fruits, labneh, whipped mascarpone or yoghurt.

Makes 8–10

225g fine semolina flour
50g plain white flour
7g sachet fast-action dried yeast
2½ tablespoons caster sugar
1½ teaspoons baking powder
a pinch of table salt
475ml lukewarm water
unsalted butter for cooking

To serve
2 large peaches, or 4 plums or
   apricots, halved, stones removed
   and the flesh quartered
20g caster sugar
1 teaspoon unsprayed dried lavender
labneh
2 tablespoons clear honey

Place the semolina, flour, yeast, sugar, baking powder and salt into a blender. Add about 100ml of the lukewarm water and blitz until the batter is smooth and silky. Add the remaining water and blitz again for a few seconds. Cover and set aside in a warm spot to prove for about 30 minutes until it becomes bubbly.

Meanwhile, preheat the oven to 200°C/Fan 180°C/Gas Mark 6.

Toss the peaches, plums or apricots in the 20g caster sugar and then transfer to an ovenproof serving dish. Bake for 15–20 minutes until softened, caramelised and the juices begin to bleed. Set aside.

Give the batter a good stir. Heat a non-stick sauté pan over a medium-high heat. Melt a little butter in the pan. When it starts to foam, pour in about 100ml to make a thin pancake. Cook steadily until the pancake sets and little bubbles and holes appear on the surface. Don't flip it.

When the pancake is set, transfer it to a plate and top with a piece of baking parchment. Repeat the process until all the batter has been used, layering the cooked pancakes.

Sprinkle the pancakes with lavender, add a dollop of labneh and drizzle with honey. Spoon the baked fruit on top and serve, with extra labneh on the side.

Chilled Watermelon and Cucumber Soup
with yoghurt and mint

This delicious, ice-cold gazpacho-style soup is ultra-refreshing and the perfect coolant in sweltering heat. During summer months, as the mercury rises, I'll make a batch to keep in a flask in the fridge ready to pour into chilled glasses for unexpected guests. Finish with fresh mint leaves, an ice cube as a float and creamy yoghurt to stir in.

Serves 4–6

750g watermelon, peeled, deseeded
   and roughly chopped
150g cherry tomatoes
1 slice day-old white bread, crusts
   removed and roughly chopped
1 cucumber, lightly peeled
   and chopped
1 garlic clove, peeled
a handful of fresh mint leaves
3 tablespoons extra virgin olive oil,
   plus extra to serve
2 tablespoons red wine vinegar
ice cubes, to serve (optional)
Greek yoghurt, to serve (optional)
sea salt and freshly ground black
   pepper

Transfer the watermelon, cherry tomatoes, bread, cucumber, garlic and half the mint leaves to a bowl. Season well, sprinkle over half the extra virgin olive oil and the vinegar and toss through.

A stand blender is ideal for this, but you can also use a food processor. You will probably have to process this in 2 or 3 batches. Transfer the watermelon mixture to a blender and blitz until very smooth. As each batch is blitzed, transfer it to another bowl. When everything has been blended, check the seasoning of the soup and adjust with salt, pepper and vinegar. Whisk in the remaining oil then transfer to a fridge to fully chill.

A half hour before serving, put individual freezerproof glasses or bowls in the freezer.

Just before serving, shred the remaining mint. Divide the soup among the glasses or bowls, then finish with some fresh mint, a drizzle of oil and an ice cube, if you wish. Serve the yoghurt on the side, if using.

Smoky Grilled Vegetables
with spiced lemon dressing

This is a North African version of the Catalonian *escalivada*, a roasted vegetable salad. *Mechouia* has a delicious spice-infused dressing that acts as a marinade for the grilled sweet vegetables. If possible, cook the vegetables over a barbecue to get the authentic smoky flavours, otherwise a really hot oven does the job nicely.

Serves 4

2 small aubergines
2 large red peppers
1 bunch large garden onions
   (bulbous spring onions)
12 vine cherry tomatoes
2 courgettes, trimmed and cut
   into long thick slices
olive oil
sea salt and freshly ground black
   pepper

For the spiced lemon dressing
1 garlic clove, peeled
1 teaspoon sea salt
50ml extra virgin olive oil
4 teaspoons harissa (page 200 or
   shop bought)
1½ teaspoons red wine vinegar, such
   as cabernet sauvignon
1 teaspoon ground caraway
1 teaspoon ground cumin
½ teaspoon smoked paprika
juice of 1 lemon

To finish
½ teaspoon caraway seeds
1 small bunch of coriander
   leaves, chopped
a handful of flat-leaf parsley
   leaves, chopped

Light a barbecue 30 minutes before you want to cook so the coals turn grey and are at the optimum temperature when you're ready to cook. Position the grill above the coals so it gets very hot. Or preheat an oven to its maximum setting. You can also use a large, ridged cast-iron griddle pan heated to the maximum for grilling the tomatoes and courgettes.

First make the dressing. I use a pestle and mortar, but you can also use a blender. Pound the garlic and salt together to make a smooth paste. Add the remaining ingredients and mix them in well. Adjust the seasoning to taste. Set aside.

Grill the aubergines, peppers and onions until they are charred and very tender all the way through. The onions will take the longest – about 30 minutes. You can add the tomatoes and courgettes to the other vegetables on the barbecue or use the searing griddle pan until they are tender and charred. Alternatively, if you are using the oven, toss the vegetables with olive oil and roast for 20 minutes to colour them. Lower the oven temperature to 200°C/Fan 180°C/Gas Mark 6, and continue roasting the vegetables until they are all tender.

As all the vegetables are cooked, transfer them to a roasting tray to catch all the juices, and leave them until cool enough to handle. Peel the charred skin from the peppers, aubergines and onions, then halve and remove the seeds from the peppers. Tear all the vegetables into strips and place in a serving bowl with the tomatoes. Pour over the resting juices, followed by the dressing. Toss well, season and sprinkle over the caraway seeds and chopped coriander and parsley.

Roasted Herb-stuffed Sardines
with aleppo pepper and lemon slices

Fresh sardines are abundant along the coastline of Morocco. Families living near the sea will eat them regularly through the week, and when the shimmering fish are at their freshest, they need very little embellishment.

This delicious way with the sardine is nothing more than an assembly of ingredients given a quick roasting in the oven. Try to source the Aleppo pepper (available online and in big supermarkets), a type of dried chilli flake that has a lovely sweet and smoky flavour with a real kick. Serve with pitta bread (page 154 or shop bought) to mop up the flavoursome oily juices left in the baking tray.

Serves 4

12 fresh large sardines, butterflied
  – a fishmonger will do this for you
12 fresh bay leaves
12 fresh thyme sprigs
a small handful of flat-leaf
  parsley leaves
a small handful of dill fronds
olive oil
sea salt
1 lemon, thinly sliced
1 teaspoon Aleppo pepper flakes

You'll need some butchers' twine or cooks' string for this. Preheat the oven to 220°C/Fan 200°C/Gas mark 7. Rinse the sardines under cold running water and pat dry.

First stuff each sardine with the herbs. Open each butterflied fish like a book, flesh side up. Place 1 bay leaf, 1 thyme sprig and a pinch each of the dill and parsley along the centre. Now fold the sides together to enclose the herbs. Tie each fish with a single piece of twine or string and a knot to secure the herbs.

You want to use an ovenproof serving dish large enough to hold the fish in a single layer. Drizzle the dish with olive oil, then nestle in the sardines. Sprinkle over plenty of sea salt and drape with the lemon slices.

Place in the oven and roast for 15–20 minutes until the sardines are just cooked – they will feel firm, and the flesh will be opaque and the skins will be lightly browned. The herbs should smell beautifully aromatic.

Remove from the oven and sprinkle over the Aleppo pepper flakes. Leave to cool for 10 minutes before serving.

Spiced Crab and Egg Briks
with coriander

Briks are delicious deep-fried, stuffed pastries found all over Morocco and Tunisia, where you'll spot them bubbling away on the street in vast wok-like pans. They are a hugely popular grab-and-go street food filled with spicy fish, meat or vegetables.

Makes 4

1 fresh red chilli, deseeded and
    finely chopped
½ teaspoon cumin seeds
1½ teaspoons coriander seeds
½ teaspoon ground cinnamon, plus
    extra for dusting
½ teaspoon ground turmeric
500g fresh white crab meat,
    picked over to remove any shell
    or cartilage
100g fresh brown crab meat, passed
    through a sieve
5 spring onions, thinly sliced
a handful of dill fronds,
    roughly chopped
a handful of flat-leaf parsley leaves,
    finely chopped
50g roasted red peppers from a jar,
    drained and finely chopped
grated zest and juice of ½
    unwaxed lemon
4 sheets of filo pastry
50g unsalted butter, melted
4 eggs
sea salt and freshly ground black
    pepper

Preheat the oven to 220°C/Fan 200°C/Gas Mark 7. Line a baking sheet with baking parchment and set aside.

Put the chilli and the cumin and coriander seeds in a pestle and mortar and pound until ground. Stir in the ground cinnamon and turmeric.

Put both the crab meats in a bowl with the mixed chilli and spices, the spring onions, dill, parsley, red peppers and lemon zest and juice. Season to taste.

Lay a sheet of filo on the work surface and brush it with melted butter. Fold in half to make a rectangle. Put one-quarter of the crab mixture in the top third of the rectangle and make a well in the centre. Crack in an egg, then fold the pastry over to encase the filling. Brush with butter, then transfer to the baking sheet. Repeat until you have 4 parcels.

Place the baking sheet in the oven and bake the briks for 15 minutes, or until golden brown and cooked through. Dust with cinnamon and serve hot.

Spice-crusted Quail
with rosewater and cucumber

Quail are hugely popular across the Mediterranean, especially in North Africa and along the eastern shores. They are wonderful when spatchcocked and cooked over a barbecue. The rose and cucumber 'sauce' has a lovely delicate cooling quality, and can also be used as a dressing for salads and roasted or grilled vegetables.

Serves 4

1 teaspoon ground allspice
1 teaspoon cumin seeds
1 teaspoon coriander seeds
½ teaspoon ground cinnamon
8 butterflied quail – a butcher
  will do this
olive oil
sea salt and freshly ground black
  pepper

For the sauce
75ml extra virgin olive oil
50ml red wine vinegar, such as
  cabernet sauvignon
25ml clear honey
1 teaspoon rosewater
½ cucumber, peeled, deseeded and
  cut into 0.5cm dice
a small handful of organic rose
  petals (optional)

Light a barbecue about 30 minutes before you want to cook so the coals turn ashen grey and are at the optimum grilling temperature. Position the grill above the coals so it gets very hot. Alternatively, heat a large ridged, cast-iron griddle pan to maximum.

Meanwhile, place the ground allspice, cumin and coriander seeds and ground cinnamon in a pestle and mortar and grind to a rough powder. Set aside.

When you are ready to cook, rub the quail with oil, season with salt and pepper and sprinkle over the spice mix. Grill for 3–4 minutes on each side to char the skins and until the meat is just cooked – a little pink tinge on the meat is fine. Remove from the grill and rest for 5 minutes.

While the quail are cooking, make the sauce. Whisk the extra virgin olive oil, vinegar, honey and rosewater together. Season well and stir in the cucumber and rose petals, if using.

Spoon the sauce over the quail and serve.

Pastilla

with slow-cooked pheasant, dates, walnuts and pistachios

The ultimate North African comfort food: a meat, fish or vegetable pie baked into a super-crisp casing of filo or *warqa* pastry. The strong gaminess of the pheasant marries beautifully with the sweet dates and almonds. Pigeon and guinea fowl also work well in this recipe.

Serves 4

olive oil
4 bone-in pheasant legs
2 garlic cloves, finely chopped
2 onions, finely chopped
1 carrot, peeled and diced
1 cinnamon stick
1 teaspoon ground ginger
a pinch of saffron threads
500ml chicken stock (fresh or
  homemade is best)
8 Medjool dates, pitted and
  roughly chopped
70g walnut halves, ground
1 large free-range egg, beaten
5 sheets filo pastry
150g unsalted butter, melted
1 tablespoon shelled pistachio
  nuts, chopped
icing sugar for dusting
a handful of fresh mint leaves,
  to garnish
sea salt and freshly ground black
  pepper

Heat a splash of olive oil in a large flameproof casserole over a medium heat. Add the pheasant legs and fry to brown slowly on both sides before adding the garlic, onions and carrot. Fry for a few minutes, stirring, until the onions are softened but without colour. Remove the pheasant legs from the casserole and set aside.

Turn the heat down to low. Add the cinnamon stick, ground ginger and saffron threads to the fat remaining in the casserole, and continue stirring for a minute or so. Return the legs to the casserole. Stir in the stock and dates and leave to simmer for 1 hour, or until the meat starts to easily come away from the bones. Remove the pheasant legs and set aside to cool.

Boil the stock over a high heat until it reduces to one-third, then add the ground walnuts, lower the heat and stir for a few minutes to thicken the sauce. Turn off the heat.

Once the sauce has cooled, whisk in the egg. Remove the meat from the leg bones and gently break into small pieces. Return to the sauce and stir in. Season and place to one side to cool completely. Remove and discard the cinnamon stick.

When the filling is cool, brush the filo pastry sheets with melted butter to stop them from drying out.

Preheat the oven to 200°C/Fan 180°C/Gas Mark 6. Use 3 sheets of filo to cover the base of a shallow, round pie dish with overhanging pastry all round.

Add the meat mix to the pie dish and ensure it is spread out evenly. Fold the overhanging filo in towards the centre. Add another sheet of buttered filo pastry to seal it fully, then top with the remaining filo sheet. I like to ruffle the top pastry sheet to give a dramatic presentation.

Place the pie dish on a baking sheet and transfer to the oven. Bake for 35 minutes, or until the pastry is crisp and becoming golden brown.

Remove the pie dish from the oven, brush over the remaining melted butter, sprinkle with the pistachios and sift over icing sugar. Return to the oven for 5–7 minutes until the pastry is fully golden brown and nicely glazed.

Leave to cool for a few minutes, then carefully transfer from the pie dish to a plate – use a metal spatula to gently ease the pastilla out of the dish. Dust with more icing sugar and sprinkle with fresh mint. It's ready to serve.

Braised Oxtail
with prunes, molasses and bay leaves

Try this deep, rich, dark pot of exotic deliciousness. This is one of my favourite recipes to cook on a chilly autumn or winter weekend, when the pressure of work is off and I want some steadying. Traditionally this type of braise is cooked gently in a tagine, though a heavy-based, ovenproof casserole with a tight-fitting lid works just fine.

Oxtail rarely makes an appearance on household menus nowadays, which is a great shame as the slow cooking yields one of the most delicious and unctuous meats around.

A bowl of fragrant, steamed couscous is the perfect accompaniment, or, when time is tight, then just serve with simple steamed basmati rice.

Serves 4 as a hearty main

1.5kg oxtail, cut into pieces (a butcher
   will do this)
a handful of plain white flour
olive oil
3 fresh or dried bay leaves
3 garlic cloves, thinly sliced
2 carrots, scrubbed and thinly sliced
2 onions, thinly sliced
1cm piece fresh root ginger, peeled
   and finely chopped
2 cinnamon sticks
1 tablespoon ground cumin
1 teaspoon ground cardamom
1 teaspoon smoked paprika
a pinch of saffron threads
400g tinned chickpeas, drained
   and rinsed
1.5 litres chicken stock (fresh
   or homemade is best)
100g pitted prunes
2 tablespoons date or
   pomegranate molasses
a small bunch of coriander, leaves
   and stalks roughly chopped
a handful of flaked almonds,
   to garnish
sea salt and freshly ground black
   pepper

Pat the oxtail pieces dry, then dredge them in the flour to lightly coat and shake off the excess. Season well.

Heat a large splash of oil in a large sauté pan over a medium heat. When it is hot, fry the floured oxtail to brown them on all sides – it's important they are nicely coloured, as this will give you a great depth of flavour. You will have to do this in batches. Set aside and add a little more oil to the pan as it is needed until all the oxtail pieces are browned.

Heat a little more oil in the same pan, still over a medium heat. Add the bay leaves, garlic, carrots, onions and ginger, and fry, stirring as you go, until the vegetables are softened and lightly browned. Now add the cinnamon sticks, ground cumin and cardamom, paprika and saffron, and stir for 2 minutes until fragrant. Add the chickpeas and stir for a further 2 minutes. Season and set aside.

If not using a tagine, preheat the oven to 160°C/Fan 140°C/Gas Mark 3.

Transfer the vegetable and chickpea mixture to the base of a tagine or a large flameproof casserole and add the oxtail pieces, including any juices. Pour in the stock. Cover with the lid and place the tagine over a low heat for 4 hours. Stir once or twice during this time and check that the liquid never reaches more than a low simmer.

If using a casserole, cover and transfer it to the oven for 4 hours, stirring once or twice and checking that the liquid never reaches more than a low simmer.

Whichever cooking container you have used, now is the time to stir in the prunes, molasses and coriander. Re-cover and leave the oxtail to rest for 10 minutes before sprinkling over the almonds. Take the tagine or casserole to the table for everyone to help themselves from.

Medjool Date and Cardamom Loaf

A sweet-savoury juicy bread to be eaten with tangy fresh labneh or thick yoghurt, accompanied by a bowl of stewed stone fruits and nuts. It's also delicious toasted and drizzled with extra virgin olive oil or just spread with salty butter.

Serves 12

1 tablespoon clear honey
500ml lukewarm water
7g sachet fast-action dried yeast
300g strong white flour, plus extra
   for kneading
150g fine semolina flour
50g ground almonds
8 green cardamom seeds, ground in a
   pestle and mortar or spice grinder
1 teaspoon table salt
olive oil for greasing the bowl
150g Medjool dates, pitted
   and chopped
date or pomegranate molasses
50g flaked almonds, toasted

Stir the honey into the lukewarm water, then stir in the yeast to dissolve. Set aside for an hour or so until it ferments and bubbles.

Mix both flours, the ground almonds, ground cardamom seeds and salt together in a large bowl. Make a well in the centre, pour in the yeast mixture and incorporate into the flour until you have a sticky dough.

Tip the dough onto a floured work surface and knead for 5–10 minutes until it is smooth and elastic. Wash, dry and grease the bowl, then return the dough to it. Cover with cling film and leave in a warm place for an hour, or until it doubles in volume.

Tip the dough onto a floured surface and knead it briefly to knock the air out. Sprinkle over the chopped dates and knead them into the dough so they are evenly distributed.

Divide the dough into 2 equal portions, then shape each into a tight ball and put them on a lightly floured baking sheet. Slash the top of each twice with a sharp serrated knife.

Cover with a tea towel and leave for about an hour until doubled in size.

Meanwhile, preheat the oven to 220°C/Fan 200°C/Gas Mark 7.

Bake the loaves for 35 minutes, or until nicely browned. Tap the bases of the loaves – they will sound hollow when baked through.

Transfer the loaves to a wire rack. Drizzle with molasses and brush to glaze the tops. Sprinkle with the toasted almonds and leave to cool completely before slicing.

Semolina and Coconut Cake
with candied rose petals

A beloved cake of North Africa, this is sultry and luxurious – one bite and you'll be instantly transported to Moroccan tea shops and souks. The semolina and coconut are not only a delicious base for a cake, but also add the most wonderful, coarse texture that is perfect for absorbing the sweet citrus syrup and heady aromas of the flower water. (I love this style of Mediterranean cake, as a lot of my recipes will testify!)

The candied rose petals are a sweet and simple addition to finish off this glorious Moroccan confection – just be sure to use unsprayed petals.

Makes 8–10 slices

100ml olive oil, plus extra for
   greasing the tin
plain white flour for dusting
410g fine semolina flour
130g desiccated coconut
2 teaspoons baking powder
1 teaspoon table salt
410g sweetened condensed milk
1 teaspoon vanilla extract
2 large free-range eggs

For the syrup
500ml water
200g caster sugar
2 tablespoons orange blossom water
2 tablespoons rosewater
finely grated zest and juice of 2
   unwaxed lemons

For the candied petals
1 large free-range egg white
petals from 2 unsprayed pink roses
130g caster sugar

First make the syrup. Combine the water, sugar, orange blossom water, rosewater and the lemon zest and juice in a small saucepan over a high heat, stirring to dissolve the sugar. Bring to the boil, then reduce the heat to medium-low and leave to simmer for 15 minutes, or until slightly reduced. Remove the syrup from the heat, pour through a sieve to remove the zest and set aside to cool completely.

Preheat the oven to 200°C/Fan 180°C/Gas Mark 6. Grease and line a 22cm springform cake tin 10cm deep, then lightly dust the base and side and tip out the excess.

Using a stand mixer, with the beater attached, mix the semolina flour with three-quarters of the coconut, the baking powder and salt until fully combined.

In a separate bowl, mix the condensed milk with the 100ml olive oil, the vanilla extract and eggs until smooth and silky. Add to the dry ingredients and mix to combine.

Transfer the batter into the prepared tin and smooth the top. Bake for about 30 minutes until the cake is golden brown and a skewer inserted in the centre comes out clean. Transfer the cake to a wire rack and drizzle half the cooled syrup over the cake. Leave the cake to stand, still in the tin, for 30 minutes, or until the syrup is fully absorbed. Pour the remaining syrup over the cake and leave until it is completely cool. Transfer the cake to the fridge and chill for 4 hours.

Meanwhile, prepare the rose petals. Line a baking sheet with baking parchment. In a small bowl, whisk the egg white until frothy. Using a pastry brush, lightly brush a rose petal with the egg white, then immediately dredge it in the caster sugar until well coated. Shake off any excess and transfer to the baking sheet. Continue until all the petals are coated and leave them to dry at room temperature for at least 4 hours.

Toast the remaining coconut at any point before serving so it has time to cool before it's used. Put it in a small sauté pan over a medium heat and toast for about 3 minutes until it is lightly browned and fragrant, tossing the pan as you go. Tip out of the pan and set aside.

When ready to serve, unmould the cake, transfer to a cake stand or plate and arrange the rose petals over the top. Sprinkle the coconut over the rose petals and cake, and it's ready to serve.

Glazed Almond Pastries
with whipped cream

These sticky and sweet fried pastries, drenched in a syrup of honey, molasses and rosewater, are typical of the rustic super-sweet desserts of North Africa. I sometimes make these in small batches as gifts for Christmas or special birthdays.

Although traditionally made with brik (or *warqa*) pastry, available in Middle Eastern food shops and online, I've used filo pastry here for convenience.

Makes 24

100g sesame seeds
12 sheets filo pastry
125g unsalted butter, melted
olive oil for frying
whipped cream, to serve

For the syrup
300ml clear honey
120ml water
100g date or pomegranate molasses
2 tablespoons lemon juice
2 teaspoons rosewater

For the filling
170g blanched almonds,
   lightly toasted
50g icing sugar
1 large free-range egg white,
   lightly beaten
2 tablespoons rosewater
½ teaspoon grated unwaxed
   orange zest

First make the syrup. Place the honey, water, molasses, lemon juice and rosewater in a saucepan over medium heat, stirring to dissolve the honey and molasses. Bring to the boil and boil for 3 minutes, without stirring, then remove from the heat and leave to cool.

To make the filling, blitz the toasted almonds in a blender until very fine. Transfer to a bowl, add the icing sugar, egg white, rosewater and orange zest, and blend well. Set aside.

Place the sesame seeds in a non-stick sauté pan over a medium heat and toast, tossing continuously, until golden and fragrant. Immediately tip them out of the pan and set aside to cool.

Fold one sheet of pastry in half horizontally, then cut into 2 long strips that are around 12cm wide and brush with melted butter. You should end up with 24 pieces.

Place 2–3 teaspoons of the almond filling at the top of each strip of pastry. Fold the top corner over the filling to form a triangle and continue folding over until the filling is completely encased in the triangle. Tuck the end corner in and place on a plate. Continue filling and shaping the triangles until all the filling and pastry are used.

Pour enough olive oil into a large, deep-sided frying pan to reach a depth of about 5cm and heat until it reaches 180°C. Check the temperature by dipping the corner of one pastry into the oil – if the oil bubbles immediately on impact, it's ready. Carefully lower in as many pastries as will fit without overcrowding the pan and fry for about 2 minutes on each side until golden brown all over.

Use a slotted spoon to remove the pastries and drop them into the syrup. Turn them in the syrup a couple of times and transfer to a serving dish. Repeat the process with the remaining pastries, making sure the oil doesn't get too hot or cool.

Once you have finished all pastries, sprinkle them with the toasted sesame seeds. Serve straightaway with the whipped cream for dipping.

islands

Crete
Sicily
Sardinia

The islands of the Mediterranean take great pride in celebrating their distinctive and singular personalities that separate them from their mainland cousins. Life is slower and the living more relaxed. The islanders' attitude to food and eating is both laid back and yet serious, with a firm focus on locality, seasonality and *terroir*. And, of course, all of life is captured, defined and influenced by the dazzling blue waters of the Mediterranean that surround them. I am an island man and the islands of the Med are the islands I love the most. Here are a few of my favourite island things.

Squid and wild pork

There are few better pleasures than spankingly fresh crispy squid, cooked for just a minute or so and then sprinkled with salt and a squeeze of lemon. It's a simple and wonderful pleasure. My best-ever calamari moment was sitting harbourside at a small port on the island of Crete eating just-caught squid, perfectly cooked, with views of a seemingly never-ending azure sea.

But Crete has more than just the bounties of the sea to offer. If you can drag yourself away from the shoreline and move inland, the delights of succulent, gamey wild pork await. It's a pleasure not to be missed and a favourite of mine when roasted to perfection outdoors over fire.

Cretan pies

It was a surprise to me to discover Crete has a tradition of making wonderful pies. The Cretan pie uses an unusual olive oil-rich pastry dough into which are piled all sorts of delicious ingredients – perhaps local cheeses, or spinach, maybe wild greens and sometimes seafood or wild game.

I love this unique pastry eccentricity that traces its origins back to the Middle Ages and the Moorish occupation. Arab cooks would make heavy pastry parcels using olive oil, stuffed with wild fennel and nettles, to be cooked overnight in primitive wood ovens until firm and crisp. The tough wild greens, slowly steamed to tenderness, were ideal for farm workers and fishermen to take out on long working days. As with the Cornish pasty, the pie acted as an ingenious, edible vessel to feed hungry workers who were separated from the luxury of kitchens and cafés. I love pasties and I love the Cretan pies.

Fennel

The wonderful sweet aniseed aroma of fennel seems to greet you everywhere you go in Sicily, and it is so versatile. My recipe for fennel, chicory, blood orange and burrata salad on page 266 is a perfect example of all of its uses. The subtle spicing of the seeds appears in many of the islands' most delicious recipes (such as Sardinia's *panne carasua* on page 280), while the flowers of the plant are often dried and sprinkled over dishes at the last moment as a seasoning, the dried fennel 'pollen' taking on an almost curry-like flavour. (My octopus recipe on page 288 uses both the fronds and the seeds for real island flavour.)

Tuna

The tuna landed in the Mediterranean and on the islands of Sardinia and Sicily is often caught in the traditional way, and it is some of the best to be found in the world. Once off the market stalls the tuna is ready to be turned into exquisite *crudo*, or perhaps grilled as steaks or even cooked pink as whole loins on a rotisserie over fire, basted regularly with olive oil infused with dried fennel. And all tasting as delicious as it sounds!

Sardinian cheese

I first fell in love with Sardinian cheese a few years back on a research trip just ahead of opening my restaurant Norma in London's Fitzrovia. Mostly the island's cheeses are hard, salty, robust and very delicious. But I discovered there are also much fresher, younger, softer varieties, often used in some of the local specialities. *Seadas*, a warm pastry stuffed with soft cheese, honey and thyme, is astonishingly delicious and sits somewhere between a pudding and a savoury. As with so much of island life it is the unexpected that surprises and delights.

Sicily

My book *Sicilia* was a long love letter to the island and to its food culture. Though Sicily and the mainland of Italy share nationhood, they differ in many other ways, not least in their styles of food. A rich Moorish culture, derived from centuries of Arab occupation, has bequeathed the island a sort of 'crossroads' food culture. The Italian passion for pasta, pizza, rice, grilled proteins and sweet things are imbued and flavoured with ingredients more associated with Arab cuisine – exotic spices, dried fruits and dramatic and flamboyant sweet desserts. This cultural culinary combination is mesmerising, addictive and bewitching.

This largest of the Mediterranean islands boasts an extraordinary menu of wonderful produce. Bulbous aubergines, incredible full-flavoured sweet tomatoes and plump grapes, all fuelled in growth and character by the island's volcanic soil and the relentless beating Sicilian sun. Fresh fish abounds. Perhaps sea bream to be grilled over coals or raw to be cured and served as crudo (page 269), or the wonderful local red *gambero rosso* prawns, just served with a drizzle of olive oil and a squeeze of lemon.

Centuries of poverty has brought a certain style of frugal creative cooking to island life. The simplest, most rustic of ingredients are magically transformed into things of staggering flamboyance and ceremony. *Timballo* is perhaps the perfect example (page 271) – it's a wonderful dish that could easily replace the majesty of a rib of beef as a stunning centrepiece.

Sicily is forever calling me and I am always making plans for the next trip to my favourite Mediterranean island.

Fried Squid
with samphire and preserved lemons

One of life's true pleasures – a plate of crispy squid served alongside an ice-cold beer, preferably somewhere by the sea where it is sunny and hot.

The Cretans know how to fry squid. Baby squid are the best when split, dipped in a coarse flour and then fried very quickly for a nice crunch and served piping hot. The preserved lemon slices are fried alongside the squid and they are a revelation, almost a standalone snack in themselves. I serve these unbeatable squid with fresh, salty samphire and an aïoli or a mayonnaise dip.

Serves 4 as a starter

400g baby squid, cleaned and cut in half, tentacles and all
500ml whole milk
4 tablespoons coarse cornmeal
4 tablespoons plain white flour
sea salt
rapeseed or sunflower oil for deep-frying
2 preserved lemons, drained and sliced (remove any pips)

To serve
30g fresh cleaned samphire
lemon wedges
aïoli (page 38 or shop bought) or mayonnaise (optional)

Place the squid in a bowl and pour over the milk. Leave for an hour or so – this helps to tenderise the flesh. Mix the cornmeal, flour and 1 teaspoon of sea salt together, then set aside.

Heat enough oil for deep-frying in a deep-fat fryer or a heavy-based saucepan until it reaches 180°C, or until a sprinkle of flour fizzles on impact.

Drain the squid well and transfer to the flour along with the preserved lemon slices. Toss through to coat and then knock off any excess.

Working in batches to avoid overcrowding the pan, add the squid and preserved lemons to the oil and fry until they are crispy and light golden brown. Drain well on a tray lined with kitchen paper and sprinkle with sea salt. Keep warm in a low oven and continue until all the squid and lemon slices are fried.

Serve in bowls with the samphire, lemon wedges for squeezing over and the aïoli, if using.

Grilled Smoky Sardines
with crushed fennel and fenugreek seeds

In the summer months throughout the Mediterranean, you'll find delicious, plump sardines sizzling away over charcoal barbecues. Some of the best sardines I've ever had were being grilled and served on the Glyka Nera beach, near the Cretan town of Loutro. The Mermaid Island Taverna juts out into the sea serving simple, fresh fish dishes and ice-cold beers. It's a spit-and-sawdust sort of place and all the better for it. There's just a lone cook grilling squid and sardines that are then served with lemon and sprinkled with a dried spice mix. There are also bottles of Hellmann's-style mayonnaise dotted all around the place.

This is my 'back-at-home-in-the-garden-in-East-London' version. You'll be able to get fresh Cornish sardines from your fishmonger from June onwards through the summer months. I don't think you can do better than to serve these with aïoli or mayonnaise and freshly fried chips.

Serves 4

2 teaspoons fennel seeds
½ teaspoon fenugreek seeds
12 large, super-fresh sardines, gutted and scaled – a fishmonger will do this for you
olive oil
a handful of fennel or dill fronds, to garnish
sea salt and freshly ground black pepper

To serve
lemon wedges
aïoli (page 38; optional), or good old Hellmann's
Holiday Chips (page 102, optional)

Light a barbecue about 30 minutes before you want to cook so the coals turn ashen grey and are at the optimum grilling temperature. Position the grill above the coals so it gets very hot. Alternatively, heat a large ridged, cast-iron griddle pan to maximum.

Crush the fennel and fenugreek seeds in a pestle and mortar until you have a fairly fine powder.

Rinse the sardines under cold running water and pat dry. Drizzle the sardines with oil and rub it all over the skin. Season well and sprinkle with half the ground seeds. Grill for 3–4 minutes on each side, turning regularly with tongs until the fish are cooked through – they will feel firm, the flesh will be opaque and the skins will be nicely charred and crispy. Set aside.

While the sardines are grilling put the lemon wedges on the grill until caramelised.

Serve the sardines with the remaining ground seeds and the fennel fronds sprinkled over and the caramelised lemon wedges alongside with aïoli and chips, as you like.

Orzo, Red Prawns, Garlic and Chillies

Orzo are the little pieces of rice-shaped pasta you encounter in dishes all over Greece. The small shape makes it ideal for bulking out soups and stews, or for being cooked risotto-style by frying and then gradually adding layers of flavours and stock.

This recipe has similarities to the Spanish paella, including the addition of a little saffron for colour and extra flavour. My introduction to this dish came from a friend who lives in Sougia, on the southern coast of Crete, where his family own a taverna and have been cooking versions of this for decades. I could never convince him to give me the recipe, so here's my take.

Serves 4

500ml fish or vegetable stock (fresh or homemade is best)
½ teaspoon saffron threads
peeled zest of ½ unwaxed orange
olive oil
250g orzo
3 garlic cloves, finely sliced
1 teaspoon fennel seeds
a pinch of dried red chilli flakes
400g tinned chopped tomatoes
2 fresh red chillies, deseeded and finely sliced
450g raw shelled *gambero rosso* or Atlantic prawns, deveined with the heads removed
a large handful of basil leaves
1 lemon, halved
sea salt and freshly ground black pepper

Put the stock, saffron and orange zest in a saucepan and leave to simmer while you get on with the rest of the recipe.

Heat a splash of oil in a large sauté pan over a medium heat. When it is hot, add the orzo, garlic, fennel seeds and chilli flakes, and fry, stirring regularly, for 3–4 minutes to coat and colour the pasta and cook the spices. Season well, then add the infused stock bit by bit, stirring as you go until the pasta absorbs the liquid.

Pour in the tomatoes and red chillies and simmer for a further 5 minutes to reduce the tomatoes and thicken the 'sauce'. Stir in the prawns, add another good splash of olive oil and throw in half the basil. Check the seasoning and add lemon juice to taste.

Turn off the heat and leave everything to rest for 2–3 minutes as the prawn flesh turns pale pink – they literally cook in the residual heat. Serve with the remaining basil scattered over the top.

Grilled Pork Chops
with fennel, figs, sage and sweet vinegar

The white wine vinegar used in the marinade is the secret to the success of this dish. The fattiness of the pork when balanced with the delicious vinegar is an inspired combination. Use a good white wine vinegar, such as chardonnay – you don't want anything too astringent, nor too sweet, as the figs will impart their natural sugars.

Fennel and sage are natural pork bedfellows. This is my twist on a classic Cretan dish for a party or wedding, when a spit roast pig is stuffed with a muddle of fennel and sage and bathed in vinegar and lemon.

Serves 4

4 pork chops with a good layer of fat
3 tablespoons semi-sweet white
   vinegar, such as chardonnay
1 tablespoon extra virgin olive oil
2 garlic cloves, thinly sliced
2 small fennel heads, halved
   lengthways
olive oil
1 teaspoon fennel seeds, lightly
   crushed in a pestle and mortar
4 fresh figs, halved lengthways
a handful of fresh sage leaves
sea salt and freshly ground black
   pepper

Place the chops in a bowl, pour over the vinegar, extra virgin olive oil and garlic, and season well. Cover and leave to marinate in the fridge for about 1 hour.

Preheat the oven to 200°C/Fan 180°C/Gas Mark 6.

Place the fennel in a large roasting tin, season well, drizzle with olive oil and sprinkle over the fennel seeds. Transfer to the oven and roast for 15 minutes. Add the figs to the tin and continue roasting for a further 15 minutes, or until the fennel is just tender and caramelised and the figs are softened. Remove the figs, set aside and keep hot. Do not turn the oven off.

Meanwhile, heat a large cast-iron griddle pan over a medium heat. Drain the chops from the marinade and pat them dry. Pour the remaining marinade into a small saucepan.

Grill the pork chops on each side for 6–7 minutes to caramelise (you might need to do this in 2 batches). Immediately transfer the chops to the roasting tin with the fennel. Sprinkle over the sage and return the tin to the oven to roast a further 7–8 minutes to cook the pork through, crisp the fat and wilt the sage.

Remove the tin from the oven and return the figs. Leave the pork to rest for about 5 minutes before serving.

While the pork is resting, bring the pork marinade to a boil for one minute, then pour over the pork, fennel and figs in the roasting tin – this combines with the resting juices to create a delicious sauce. Serve.

Slow-cooked Lamb Shoulder
with spinach, dill and lemon

This is my spin on the Cretan classic of lamb with dill and lemon sauce. What I love about this dish is its seasonal versatility. It's wonderful in the winter, but also perfect in the spring due to the freshness imparted by the zingy lemon and the fresh, vibrant spinach and dill. A lamb shoulder cut is perfect for this kind of slow cooking, holding its shape and flavour with just the right amount of tasty fat to enrich the sauce.

This is a favourite Sunday treat in the Tish household. A one-pot wonder and so much easier to make than a traditional Sunday roast with all its time-consuming moving parts. A dollop of Greek yoghurt added when serving is a nice touch.

Serves 4–6

olive oil
2 tablespoons plain white flour
800g piece boneless lamb shoulder,
    cut into 4 equal chunks and
    patted dry
4 garlic cloves, thinly sliced
2 bay leaves
1 cinnamon stick
1 large glass of dry white wine
700ml chicken stock (fresh or
    homemade is best)
100g new potatoes, scrubbed and
    cut into 0.5cm slices
grated zest and juice of 1
    unwaxed lemon
100g spinach leaves, washed
fronds from a small bunch of dill
Greek yoghurt, to serve (optional)
sea salt and freshly ground black
    pepper

Heat a large splash of olive oil in a large flameproof casserole over a medium heat.

Put the flour in a bowl and season with salt and pepper. Dredge the lamb pieces in the flour and shake off any excess. When the oil is hot, transfer the pieces to the casserole and fry on all sides until nicely browned and caramelised.

Add the garlic, bay leaves and cinnamon stick, and fry, stirring, for a minute or so. Add the wine and boil until it is nearly evaporated, scraping the bottom of the pan with a wooden spatula to release any sediment.

Pour in the stock and return to the boil. Lower the heat and leave to simmer, partially covered, for 30 minutes. Skim off any foam on the surface of the stock, then add the potatoes and lemon juice. Continue simmering for a further 35 minutes, or until the lamb is meltingly tender, the potatoes soft and the cooking liquor has reduced to a sauce consistency – if it's too thick, add some water to loosen. Turn off the heat, season well and rest for at least 30 minutes, partially covered.

When you are ready to serve, bring the dish back to a simmer and stir in the spinach and half the dill. Check the seasoning again and then divide among 4 bowls. Finish with the lemon zest, the remaining dill and a dollop of yoghurt, if using.

Spinach, Fennel and Herb Pie

I love this Cretan-style pie with its rich and crumbly olive oil-based crust. I've eaten many versions on my travels and the options for predominantly vegetable-based fillings are plentiful – courgettes, kale, green cabbage and even diced squash or pumpkin. Aleppo-style pepper and cumin are also often used in the spicing.

Sesame seeds are regularly used in Cretan cuisine, a legacy of its Moorish occupation, adding a sweet, caramelly nuttiness to the pie crust when baked, which I very much like.

Serves 8

100ml olive oil
2 fennel heads, finely chopped
2 red onions, finely chopped
1 leek, washed and finely chopped
a bunch of spring onions,
    finely chopped
1 teaspoon fennel seeds
500g spinach, washed and
    finely chopped
fronds from a bunch of dill,
    roughly chopped
leaves from a bunch of mint,
    roughly chopped
100g feta, drained and crumbled
2 large free-range eggs, beaten
sea salt and freshly ground black
    pepper

For the pastry

500g plain white flour, sifted, plus
    extra for rolling out
1 teaspoon table salt
200ml olive oil, plus extra for
    greasing the pie dish
200ml lukewarm water
1 large free-range egg, beaten, to glaze
2 tablespoons sesame seeds

Heat the olive oil in a large saucepan over a medium heat. When it is hot, add the fennel, red onions, leek, spring onions and fennel seeds, and season. Turn the heat down to medium-low and leave to sweat for 30–35 minutes until softened but without colour. Stir often as you go to avoid anything sticking. When everything is softened, turn off the heat and stir in the spinach, dill and mint. Season again.

Let the vegetables cool completely before stirring in the crumbled feta and eggs. Set aside at room temperature.

Meanwhile, make the pastry. Place the flour and salt in a bowl. Make a well in the centre, add the olive oil and water and gradually work this into the flour to form a soft dough. Don't overwork the dough as it can become heavy. Cover and chill for 30 minutes.

Preheat the oven to 200°C/Fan 180°C/Gas Mark 6. Grease a round 25–30cm pie dish.

Lightly dust a work surface with flour and then cut the dough into 2 pieces – you want one piece slightly larger for the pie base. Roll out the larger piece in a circular motion until it is about 0.5cm thick, dusting with more flour as you go. Fold it over the rolling pin and then roll into the pie dish. Press the pastry into the side well, leaving an overhang. Spoon in the vegetable and feta filling and spread it out evenly.

...continued on page 258

Roll out the remaining pastry until 0.5cm thick and lay over the top of the filling. Pinch the pastry edges together to seal the pie, then trim off the excess pastry. Brush the top with beaten egg, sprinkle over the sesame seeds and poke a couple of holes in the top to let out excess steam.

Place the pie dish on a baking sheet and transfer it to the oven. Bake for 1 hour, or until the pastry is golden brown and crisp. Leave to stand for at least 5 minutes before serving. It's equally good served hot or at room temperature.

Rice Pudding
with sultanas and sticky dates

Usually served cold, this dessert is actually cooked risotto-style, simmered slowly and constantly stirred to help the starch transfer from the rice into the creamy sauce and to avoid the rice catching and burning. There are many variations on rice pudding to be found throughout the Mediterranean. I have written recipes inspired by rice puddings from Italy, Spain and France, and I continue to be on the lookout for great local versions on my travels. This version from Crete sets itself apart from others with its much wetter consistency, almost custard-like, and is usually served cold. Flavourings might include allspice, green cardamoms or orange flower water. This is seriously delicious and wonderfully comforting.

Serves 6

75g sultanas
250g short-grain pudding rice
300ml water
900ml whole milk
200g caster sugar
2 cinnamon sticks
peeled zest of 1 unwaxed orange
a pinch of sea salt
6 Medjool dates, pitted and
   roughly chopped
2 large free-range egg yolks, beaten
a few drops of rosewater
2 teaspoons ground cinnamon

Place the sultanas in a small bowl, cover with lukewarm water and leave to soak for 20 minutes. When they are plump and tender, drain them well.

Meanwhile, place the rice and water in a saucepan over a medium heat, stirring continuously until the rice has absorbed all the water, as if you were making a risotto. This should take 15 minutes or so.

In a separate pan, mix the milk, sugar, cinnamon sticks and orange zest together, and warm through over a low heat, stirring as you go.

Pour the warm milk onto the rice with the salt. Simmer, stirring constantly, until the rice has absorbed all the milk, which will take another good 15 minutes or so. Stir in the drained sultanas and Medjool dates.

Remove the pan from the heat and leave the rice pudding to cool for 10 minutes before stirring in the egg yolks and a few drops of rosewater. The consistency should be rich and thick. If it's too stodgy, you can always add a splash more milk. You can eat the pudding at this stage with great joy, or chill it for later. Sprinkle over the cinnamon if eating now.

For eating later, transfer the rice pudding into individual bowls and cover the surfaces with cling film to prevent skins forming. Leave to cool, then transfer to a fridge to chill for up to 12 hours. Sprinkle over the ground cinnamon before serving.

Cherries and Bay Leaves
in syrup

Yet another example of a preserving method turning out to be a culinary delight. In Crete preserved cherries are served to visitors alongside a cup of coffee or tea. Make a large batch of this recipe at the end of the cherry season when they are cheap and at their juiciest – supermarkets often sell off boxes at cut-down prices just to get rid of them. Multiply the other recipe ingredients accordingly. These are very, very good spooned over ice cream!

Serves 8–10

500ml full-bodied red wine
150g caster sugar
4 bay leaves
peeled zest of ½ unwaxed orange
500g plump cherries, pitted

Put the wine, sugar, bay leaves and orange zest in a saucepan over a medium heat, and slowly bring to a boil, stirring every now and then to dissolve the sugar. Add the cherries, reduce the heat and leave to simmer for 8–10 minutes until the cherries are tender, but still holding their shape.

Use a slotted spoon to transfer the cherries to a heatproof bowl. Bring the poaching liquid back to a boil and reduce by one third until it is syrupy.

Pour the reduced syrup over the cherries and leave them to macerate for at least 24 hours before serving. The cherries will keep in the syrup in an airtight container in the fridge for up to 4 weeks.

Grilled Violet Artichokes
with cumin seeds, garlic and vinegar

Palermo, the beating vibrant heart of Sicily, has the most fascinating and exciting street markets, akin to North African souks. Here you enter a world of hustle and bustle, haggling and bartering set amidst an explosion of colours, sounds and smells. Venturing deep into the market's streets you walk past clouds of smoke billowing from makeshift barbecues stacked with young artichokes slowly caramelising over the fire. These are the ultimate Sicilian street food – the cooked artichokes are doused in olive oil and lemon juice, sprinkled with parsley and then wrapped in paper to take away.

Young artichokes are available in spring. The best ones have crisp, vibrant dark green outer leaves and a pale, white tender heart tinged with purple.

Serves 4

12 young fresh small artichokes,
   ends trimmed
juice of 1 lemon
75ml extra virgin olive oil
3 garlic cloves, finely sliced
2 teaspoons cumin seeds
75ml red wine vinegar, such as
   cabernet sauvignon
olive oil
a handful of flat-leaf parsley leaves,
   roughly chopped
sea salt and freshly ground black
   pepper

Light a barbecue about 30 minutes before you want to cook so the coals turn ashen grey and are at the optimum grilling temperature. Position the grill above the coals so it gets very hot. Alternatively, heat a large ridged, cast-iron griddle pan to maximum.

Prepare the artichokes by taking off any hard outer leaves or spiky bits, then cut each in half lengthways and remove the tough central core. As they are prepared, rub them all over with lemon juice – this will stop them discolouring.

Heat the extra virgin olive oil in a small saucepan over a medium heat. When it is hot, add the garlic and cumin seeds – the seeds will start to pop and the garlic will turn a light brown. Remove the pan from the heat, then add the vinegar and seasoning. Leave to cool.

Dab the artichokes on a paper towel, then drizzle with olive oil and season well. Place on the grill over the coals and cook for 7–8 minutes, turning several times until the artichokes are tender and have a nice even caramelisation with a little char.

Transfer the artichokes to a serving dish. Stir the parsley into the vinaigrette and then pour it over them. Serve.

Spiced Roasted Pumpkin Soup
with pangrattato and sage

A hot Sicilian soup is hardly authentic, but the flavours and spirit within the soup most certainly are. The sweet-sour edge to the pumpkin is very Sicilian, while finishing the soup with some crunchy olive oil-fried breadcrumbs and crispy sage leaves makes a delicious textural contrast. I always go for a heavier pumpkin variety, such as iron bark or Delicia – their dense flesh has a much sweeter, less watery texture and flavour, and makes a rich, silky soup.

I like to shower my hot soup with freshly grated hard cheese, such as Parmesan, pecorino or *asagio* – it's your choice.

Serves 4

1.2kg pumpkin (see introduction, above), peeled, deseeded and diced
2 garlic cloves, chopped
2 shallots, finely chopped
1 tablespoon caster sugar
olive oil
50ml red wine vinegar, such as cabernet sauvignon
1 litre vegetable stock (fresh or homemade is best)
1 large slice day-old sourdough bread, broken into rustic breadcrumbs
a handful of sage leaves
50g cheese, such as pecorino, Parmesan or *asagio*, finely grated, to serve
sea salt and freshly ground black pepper

Preheat the oven to 190°C/Fan 170°C/Gas Mark 5.

Place the pumpkin in a roasting tray with the garlic and shallots, then toss with the sugar and olive oil and season well. Place in the oven to roast for 1 hour, or until the pumpkin is caramelised and tender.

Remove from the oven and place the roasting tray on the hob. Turn the heat to maximum, add the vinegar and bring to the boil, scraping the base of the tray to start to release the sediment. When the vinegar is nearly evaporated, add the stock and scrape again. Return to the boil and leave to bubble for 3 minutes.

Transfer the pumpkin and stock to a blender and blitz until smooth and silky. The soup will be quite thick – if you'd like it thinner, just add some hot water.

Transfer the soup to a saucepan, season and keep warm over a low heat.

Heat a good splash of olive oil in a sauté pan over a high heat. When it is hot, toss in the breadcrumbs and fry them, turning and tossing them, until they are golden brown and crisp. Add the sage leaves and continue to fry for 1 minute or so to crisp up.

To serve, divide among 4 bowls and top with the crispy breadcrumbs and sage. Serve with a bowl of the cheese on the table for everyone to help themselves.

Olive Oil-braised Courgettes
with almonds, mint and red chillies

Italy holds the courgette in very high esteem and grows many delicious varieties. When buying courgettes look out for the best and remember the golden rule – the heavier the courgette, the less water within and the greater the flavour.

Here is a very good way to cook courgettes; slowly in their own juices with good fruity olive oil, finished with herbs, chillies and crunchy almonds. The olive oil soaks into the courgettes, which eventually collapse into a delicious, soft, silky oblivion. This is very good when served as a side dish with roasted meats and fish, or with polenta and mashed potatoes for a vegetarian option.

Serves 4–6 as a side

extra virgin olive oil (not too peppery)
500g mixed courgettes, such as heavy
   English green, yellow, trombetta,
   Romano and grezzina, washed and
   cut into 0.5cm slices
2 large fresh red chillies, deseeded
   and finely sliced
juice of 1 lemon
a large handful of mint leaves
a handful of toasted flaked almonds,
   to serve
sea salt and freshly ground black
   pepper

Pour enough extra virgin olive oil into a heavy-bottomed saucepan to cover the base entirely, probably about 100ml, and warm gently over a medium heat.

Pile in the courgettes and stir to coat them in the oil. Cover the pan, then reduce the heat to as low as possible and leave to gently cook for 15–20 minutes until very tender. The courgettes should begin to melt into each other when stirred.

Remove the pan from the heat. Add the chillies, lemon juice and mint, and season well. Stir through again and leave to rest for a few minutes before serving. Sprinkle over the almonds and it's ready to serve.

Fennel, Chicory, Blood Orange and Burrata Salad

A fresh and vibrant salad to shine through the dark winter months when ruby-tinged blood oranges are in season and bitter Italian leaves are at their best. There are many colourful varieties of bitter leaves, from curly leaved Tardivo radicchio and the red-white rocket-shaped Treviso radicchio, to the more familiar radicchio and creamy white chicory. My list below is more suggestive than prescriptive – use as much variety as you can find.

Burrata, the creamier, more luxurious cousin of the mozzarella, is the star of this dish. The burrata must be very fresh and is now widely available at good delis and bigger supermarkets.

Serves 4

1 teaspoon coriander seeds
½ teaspoon fennel seeds
1 head red or white chicory, trimmed
    and separated into leaves
1 head Treviso radicchio, Tardivo
    radicchio, or radicchio, trimmed
    and separated into leaves
½ small head fennel, very finely sliced
    with a mandoline or sharp knife
1 blood orange, peeled and segmented
a small handful of fennel or
    dill fronds
4 x 100g very fresh burrata
sea salt and freshly ground black
    pepper

For the vinaigrette
5 tablespoons extra virgin olive oil
2 tablespoons red wine vinegar
20g clear honey

To make the vinaigrette, whisk the extra virgin olive oil, vinegar and honey together, then season and set aside.

Toast the coriander and fennel seeds in a small, dry sauté pan over a medium heat, tossing a few times. When the seeds start to smell fragrant and pop, they are ready. Immediately stir them into the vinaigrette.

Place the chicory and radicchio leaves in a mixing bowl. Add the fennel, orange segments and fennel fronds. Season well and spoon in two-thirds of the vinaigrette. Toss together and then divide the leaves and orange among individual dishes. Top each with a burrata and season with a sprinkle of salt and a grind of pepper, then spoon over the remaining vinaigrette. Serve.

Sea Bream Crudo
with blood orange and cumin seeds

This beautiful, vibrant *crudo* will brighten up the winter months when blood oranges are at their best. The bittersweet, ruby-red juices lightly cure the fish, and the cumin-infused dressing adds an earthy, aromatic punch. Always choose the freshest possible fish for *crudo*, so the just-caught sweetness and texture of the flesh stand out among the accompanying flavours.

I like to serve a platter of this in the centre of the table to share, accompanied with really good bread to mop up the citrusy, oily juices.

Serves 4

2 sea bream fillets, skinned and cut into 1cm slices
1 small blood orange (or a bitter orange, such as Seville), skin and pith removed
2 tablespoons extra virgin olive oil
½ teaspoon cumin seeds, lightly crushed in a pestle and mortar
2 tablespoons sweet white wine vinegar, such as chardonnay
1 teaspoon caster sugar
a handful of mint leaves, to garnish
sea salt and freshly ground black pepper

Place the sea bream slices in a non-metallic bowl and season well.

Segment the blood orange with a sharp knife, working over the bowl that the fish is in – you want the juices to marinate the fish. Give the sea bream a stir, then leave for 10 minutes to cure.

Heat the olive oil and cumin seeds in a small saucepan over a low heat. When the seeds start to slowly fizzle, remove the pan from the heat. Whisk in the vinegar with the sugar and season with salt and pepper.

To serve, pile the *crudo* and blood orange onto a serving platter, drizzle over a little of the cumin vinaigrette and top with the mint leaves. Serve the remaining vinaigrette alongside in case anyone wants extra.

Slow-cooked Cuttlefish
with olives, tomatoes, garlic and red wine

I have very fond memories of eating robust Sicilian cuttlefish ragouts. Seaside cafés in Cefalù are famed for their cuttlefish dishes, where pots of bubbling seafood stews steam and simmer away outside the town's kitchens. After long, slow cooking cuttlefish yield a rich, creamy meat that stands up very well to big flavours.

This ragout is lovely on its own, but also great when tossed with pasta and sublimely satisfying when piled on slabs of grilled focaccia. I'd even go as far as to grate some hard salty cheese over the top, Bolognese style.

You can also cook cuttlefish quickly in a pan or over a grill, but it can be chewy, so I recommend freezing the fish first and then defrosting to help tenderise. A friendly fishmonger will do all the fiddly prepping and cleaning for you.

Serves 4

1kg cuttlefish, cleaned and cut into bite-sized pieces or strips (cleaned frozen cuttlefish works well in this recipe – just defrost it first)
olive oil
2 garlic cloves, crushed
1 onion, finely chopped
2 tablespoons tomato purée
3 fresh bay leaves
150ml full-bodied red wine, such as nero d'avola
300ml fish stock (fresh or homemade is best)
400g plum tomatoes, chopped
75g green pitted olives, halved
leaves from a large handful of flat-leaf parsley, finely chopped
a pinch of dried chilli flakes
sea salt and freshly ground black pepper

Pat the cuttlefish dry. Heat a good splash of olive oil in a large flameproof casserole over a medium heat. When it is hot, add the cuttlefish, season and fry for 3–4 minutes, stirring frequently, to obtain a little colour on the flesh. Now add the garlic and onion and continue to fry for a further 3–4 minutes to soften the onion. Stir in the tomato purée with the bay leaves and keep stirring for a minute or so to cook out the tomato purée. Stir in the wine and boil to reduce by three-quarters.

Add the stock and leave to simmer, uncovered, for 30 minutes, or until the stock reduces to a saucy consistency. Add the chopped tomatoes and keep simmering over a very low heat for a further 30–40 minutes until the tomatoes have broken down into the sauce and have created a delicious, rich ragout. Turn off the heat, stir in the olives, parsley and chilli flakes, and season. Cover and leave to rest for at least 20 minutes before serving. Make sure it is hot before serving.

Veal Timballo
with wild mushrooms and pecorino

The Sicilian *timballo* manages to use the simplest rustic ingredients, often leftovers, and transform them into a celebratory, extravagant culinary centrepiece. Over many centuries, Sicilian food culture has developed the gift of making a little go a long way and in the process managed to create wonderful, delicious and exciting dishes to savour.

The *timballo* – essentially a pressed savoury gâteau or cake – comes in many guises. Most *timballi* use cooked pasta or rice as the predominant filling, adding a selection of meats, cheeses, eggs and vegetables, which are then layered resplendently. They can also come encased in vegetables, such as aubergines or courgettes, or even in a type of shortcrust pastry akin to a classic British savoury pie.

I love using aubergines as an exterior case for the *timballi*, which I've done here. They are not only delicious, but also look very impressive – caramelised and carefully overlapped, glistening with olive oil. Once you've got the general hang of making *timballi*, experiment with additional fillings and flavours.

Serves 6–8

olive oil
2 carrots, peeled and finely chopped
2 garlic cloves, finely chopped
1 onion, finely chopped
30g wild mushrooms, trimmed,
   cleaned and sliced
300g minced veal (rose veal is very
   good here and more ethical)
100g minced pork
250ml full-bodied red wine
400g tinned chopped tomatoes
6 large free-range eggs
130g small dried pasta, such as
   anelletti (little pasta rings), ziti
   or pennette
50g aged pecorino cheese, grated
a handful of sage leaves, chopped
2 aubergines, cut lengthways into
   0.5cm slices
a handful of flat-leaf parsley leaves,
   to garnish
sea salt and freshly ground black
   pepper

First start the ragout. Heat a good splash of olive oil in a large flameproof casserole over a medium heat. When it is hot, add the carrots, garlic, onion and mushrooms, and cook gently, stirring occasionally, until the onion is softened but without colour.

Add the minced veal and minced pork and fry, stirring, until well browned. Add the red wine and stir well, scraping the bottom of the pan to release any sediment. When the wine has evaporated, stir in the tomatoes, cover the casserole and simmer over a low heat for 50 minutes, stirring occasionally so it doesn't catch. Season well, and continue simmering for 10 minutes, or until it is thick and rich. Turn off the heat. You can do this up to a day ahead.

Meanwhile, soft boil the eggs. Bring a large saucepan of water to the boil. Gently lower in the eggs and let them simmer for 7 minutes. Drain them in a sieve, then run cold running water over them to stop the cooking. When they are cool enough to handle, shell them and set aside.

Also while the ragout is simmering, preheat the oven to 220°C/ Fan 200°C/Gas Mark 7. Use olive oil to generously grease a non-stick 20–23cm Bundt tin, *timballo* tin or a regular springform cake tin 10cm deep. If you are using a springform tin, line the base with baking parchment cut to fit.

...continued on page 272

Bring a large saucepan of water to the boil for cooking the pasta. Once it starts to boil, add salt, then add the pasta and boil for 3 minutes less than the packet instructions. Drain well, then drizzle with olive oil.

Mix the cooked pasta and ragout together, then stir in the pecorino and sage.

Lay the aubergine slices on a roasting tray and drizzle liberally with olive oil – aubergines soak up oil like a sponge. Transfer to the oven and roast until golden brown. Transfer to kitchen paper to drain and season with salt and pepper.

Line the base and side of the mould with the aubergine slices, positioned so they are overlapping and the surface is fully covered. Cut slices to cover the base – these will be on top when the *timballo* is turned out. Now fill the mould with half the meat and pasta ragout, followed by the eggs and then the other half of the ragout. Press down with the back of a spoon to ensure it is nicely packed in.

Place the mould on a baking sheet and bake for 30 minutes. Remove from the oven and leave to cool for at least 40 minutes before inverting onto a serving plate and removing the mould. Peel off the lining paper if you used a springform tin. Sprinkle the parsley over and cut into slices to serve.

Slow-cooked Beef Cheeks in Nero d'Avola
with bread and pecorino dumplings

This is essentially beef and dumplings given a Sicilian-style twist. Beef cheeks are wonderful for long, gentle braising. They are not only flavoursome, but also hold their shape through the cooking process and have a unique, unctuous texture. I like to use a red Sicilian nero d'avola wine to give an authentic depth to the dish, but a good bottle of what you have around will work just as well.

The dumplings, known as *accussi* in the Sicilian dialect, are lovely as a dish on their own in a simple meat or chicken broth. I use my leftover sourdough or focaccia for this, but any white bread will suffice, and you can swap the ground almonds with ground walnuts for an earthier flavour.

Serves 4 as a main course or as part of a feast; makes 16 dumplings

4 small beefs cheeks, about 250g
  each, sinew removed
500ml full-bodied red wine, such as
  nero d'avola
3 fresh bay leaves
2 garlic cloves, crushed
4 shallots, halved lengthways
olive oil
700ml beef stock (fresh or
  homemade is best)
1 cinnamon stick
400ml tinned chopped tomatoes
peeled zest of ½ unwaxed orange
sea salt and freshly ground black
  pepper

For the bread dumplings (accussi)
125g day-old bread, such as sourdough
  or focaccia, broken into pieces
100ml whole milk, lukewarm
20g ground almonds
20g pecorino or Parmesan
  cheese, grated
20g plain white flour, plus extra
  for rolling
1 large free-range egg, beaten
¼ teaspoon ground nutmeg
a small handful of flat-leaf parsley
  leaves, finely chopped

Put the cheeks in a dish and cover with the wine, bay leaves, garlic and shallots. Marinate for at least 6 hours or up to 24 hours.

Meanwhile, make the dumplings. Soak the bread in the milk for 30 minutes or so to completely soften – pressing with the back of a spoon once or twice. Now add the ground almonds, cheese, flour, egg, nutmeg and parsley, and season very well. Mix to form a soft dough. Now divide the mixture into 16 equal portions and use floured hands to roll into rough balls. Place in the fridge, cover and chill until the cheeks finish marinating.

Remove the beef cheeks from the marinade, pat dry and set aside. Transfer the liquid into a large flameproof casserole over a high heat and boil the marinade until it reduces by three-quarters.

Preheat the oven to 150°C/Fan 130°C/Gas Mark 2.

Heat a splash of oil in a large sauté pan over another high heat. When it is hot, add the beef cheeks and brown for 4 minutes on each side, or until caramelised. You will most likely have to do this in batches, so transfer the cheeks to the reducing marinade as they are browned.

When the marinade is reduced, pour in the stock and add the cinnamon. Return to the boil and add the chopped tomatoes.

Cover and transfer the casserole to the oven for about 2 hours, then stir in the orange zest. Re-cover the casserole and continue cooking for a further 1½ hours, or until the cheeks are soft and tender. Skim the surface every so often to remove any fat. Season to taste, set aside and keep hot.

Bring a large pan of salted water to a boil. Gently lower the bread dumplings in and let them simmer until they begin to float. Remove with a slotted spoon and shake off any excess water. Transfer to a plate and drizzle with olive oil.

Either divide the cheeks and sauce among individual bowls or place in one large bowl to share. Nestle the dumplings between the cheeks and into the sauce, then serve.

Damson or Plum Granita
with whipped cream

This recipe was born out of the damson glut I have every year in my east London garden. It's quite astonishing how a lone damson tree can produce so much fruit year in and year out. I usually ship buckets of my damsons out to our restaurants and neighbours and then frantically try to think of ways to use up the many I am still left with in recipes at home for jams, pickles and tarts.

The colour of this fabulous ice is a sultry seductive pink that will brighten up any grey autumn day. A dollop of whipped cream is an authentic and indulgent addition.

Serves 10–12

1.2kg ripe purple plums or damsons, rinsed, halved and stones removed
100ml water
200g caster sugar
a pinch of table salt
2 tablespoons vodka or lemon juice
200ml double cream, whipped to soft peaks, to serve

Put the plum halves in a blender and purée. Set aside.

Heat the water in a small saucepan with the sugar and salt, stirring until the sugar dissolves. Add to the purée with the vodka or lemon juice and blitz again. Transfer this mixture to a freezerproof container and place in the freezer for a couple of hours until it is partially frozen.

Use a fork to scrape the frozen mixture from the edges of the container towards the centre and to scrape the surface. Return to the freezer for another hour. Repeat the scraping process a couple of times, then leave the granita in the freezer until it is softly frozen like driven freshly fallen snow. It can remain at this servable stage in the freezer for 3–4 hours, but after that the ice will become too solid. If it gets too hard, remove the container from the freezer to defrost a little, then scrape again and return to the freezer.

Serve with whipped cream.

Colomba Cake
with pistachio buttercream and rosewater

The Colomba cake is a traditional Italian Easter treat that straddles both bread and cake depending on how you dress it up and serve it. My version is firmly rooted in the cake camp and has a distinctly Sicilian flavour with the addition of a rose-scented, whipped pistachio buttercream filling.

You'll see Colomba cakes in Italian delis sitting alongside the panettones, wrapped in dove-shaped paper moulds to represent peace and a new beginning. If you make them at home, you'll find the experience very rewarding and pleasantly therapeutic. It is a fun weekend baking adventure that requires time and some careful planning. You can buy metal and paper dove moulds online, or simply use a 22cm springform cake tin 10cm deep.

Makes 10–12 slices

For the starter
30g plain white flour
1 teaspoon fast-action dried yeast
65ml lukewarm water

For the first dough
250g strong white flour
65g unsalted butter, softened, plus
   extra for the tin
60g caster sugar
90ml lukewarm water
50g starter (see above)
2 large free-range egg yolks, beaten

For the second dough
100g strong white flour
50g caster sugar
1 tablespoon clear honey
grated zest of ½ unwaxed lemon
grated zest of ½ unwaxed orange
2 large free-range egg yolks
1 teaspoon table salt
100g unsalted butter, softened
   and chopped
4 teaspoons lukewarm water
200g candied orange zest (quality
   shop-bought diced is ideal)

Start with the first dough the day before you need it – it needs all night to rise properly. First make the starter. Mix the flour and yeast together in a bowl, then whisk in the water. Leave for about 30 minutes until it starts to bubble.

For the first dough, mix the strong white flour, butter, sugar, water and 50g of the starter together in a stand mixer fitted with the dough hook. Mix for 15 minutes on low speed until you have a smooth dough that comes away clean from the sides of the bowl. Add the yolks and keep mixing until you have a fully smooth and elastic dough. Cover and leave to rise for 12 hours, or until it has tripled in volume.

After the dough has risen, knock it back to make the second dough. Add the additional 100g strong white flour to the first batch. Transfer it back to the stand mixer and knead for 10 minutes. When the dough is smooth and elastic again, mix in the sugar, honey and fresh citrus zests until well combined.

Add one of the egg yolks with the salt and mix well until fully combined. Gradually mix in the butter, mixing well between each addition, then continue kneading until the dough comes away cleanly from the sides of the bowl. Add the remaining egg yolk and mix again, then add the water. Continue mixing until the dough is smooth and glossy. Finally, mix in the candied orange until fully incorporated.

Grease a metal or paper dove cake mould or use a greased and lined 22cm springform cake tin 10cm deep. Transfer the dough into the mould, gently pressing into the mould's shape. Cover with a tea towel and leave to rise for 3 hours, or until the dough rises to the edge of the tin.

For the icing
1 egg white
½ teaspoon cornflour
25g caster sugar
1 tablespoon pearl sugar
30g shelled pistachio nuts, chopped

For the pistachio buttercream
225g unsalted butter, softened
250g icing sugar
80g pistachio paste
1 teaspoon rosewater
a pinch of table salt

Preheat the oven to 200°C/Fan 180°C/Gas Mark 6.

While the oven is heating, whisk the egg white with the cornflour to make the icing. When the dough has risen, brush the icing over the surface, then sprinkle over the caster sugar, pearl sugar and pistachios. Transfer to the oven and bake for 40–45 minutes until golden brown and a skewer inserted into the middle comes out clean. Transfer to a wire rack and leave to cool completely.

While the cake is cooling, make the buttercream. Place the butter in the bowl of a stand mixer, with the beater attached, and whisk on low speed until light and fluffy. Whisk in the icing sugar, pistachio paste, rosewater and salt. Set aside.

When the cake is cool, remove it from the mould. Use a bread knife to slice the cake in half horizontally. Spread the buttercream across the bottom half, then replace the top. Serve.

Panne Carasua
with fennel seeds and sea salt

I was first introduced to this extraordinary bread at London's Al Duca restaurant in the mid-nineties by chef Michele Franzolin. I'd never seen anything like it! It was thrown onto the chargrill for a fabulous smoky flavour, and I was instantly hooked by this Sardinian classic.

Otherwise known as *carta di musica*, or music paper bread, it is traditionally rolled as thin as paper before baking. Its origins are ancient – the original bread was created by shepherds who would spend long periods away from home and needed something that could last weeks without spoiling. The bread was either reheated over an open fire to freshen or added to soups and broths to rehydrate.

A baking stone is ideal for this recipe, but a sturdy baking sheet will work nearly as well. This recipe will keep for weeks, but I recommend giving it a blast in a very hot oven before using.

I love eating this with antipasti. It is an ideal vessel for carrying cheeses, *salumi* and pickles. I've also used it in a lasagne instead of pasta – try it!

Makes 7 sheets

250g fine semolina flour
220g plain white flour, plus extra
   for kneading and shaping
1 teaspoon baking powder
1½ teaspoons fennel seeds,
   lightly crushed
1 teaspoon table salt
350ml lukewarm water
extra virgin olive oil and sea salt,
   to serve

Mix the semolina and white flours, the baking powder, 1 teaspoon of fennel seeds, salt and water together in a large mixing bowl with your hands until everything comes together and forms a firm, elastic dough. Cover with a damp cloth and leave to rest for 20 minutes at room temperature. It will start to rise.

Turn out the dough on a floured surface, knock back and knead for about 10 minutes until it begins to spring back when pressed. Cover with a damp cloth and leave to rest again for at least 20 minutes until it starts to bubble.

Meanwhile, preheat the oven to 240°C/Fan 220°C/Gas Mark 9 with a baking stone on the middle rack. If you don't have a stone, use a large baking sheet lined with several sheets of parchment paper.

After the dough has rested, divide it into 7 equal pieces and roll them under the palm of your hand on the lightly floured work surface until they become smooth balls.

...continued on page 282

Working with one ball at a time, dip it into the white flour and shake off the excess. Using the palm of your hand, flatten the dough, then use a rolling pin to start rolling it out. Turn it 180 degrees between each roll so it becomes a long oval. Roll it as thin as you can. Using a fork, prick the dough all over. Continue until all the dough is rolled out, flouring the surface as necessary.

In batches, place the dough ovals on the baking stone or lined baking sheets and bake for 3 minutes. Use your fingers to flip each one over and bake for a further 2 minutes, or until the bread is a light golden and crisp – work quickly so you don't burn your fingertips. Continue until all the breads are baked.

Remove the breads from the stone or baking sheet and immediately brush the pieces of bread with extra virgin olive oil and sprinkle with sea salt and the remaining crushed fennel seeds, then put on a wire rack to cool slightly. Serve or save for later. A quick refresh in a very hot oven will bring them back to life.

Bitter Leaves

with baked and fresh grapes, bottarga and grape molasses

This is a wonderful salad that I make in both the summer and the winter months – a riot of tastes, textures and colours that elevates a simple salad to the ethereal. The key is to use the best variety of bitter leaves you can find.

The heady mix of salty bottarga and sweet-sour grape molasses is a typical Sardinian flavour combination. Look for grape molasses online and in Middle Eastern food shops.

Serves 4

1½ heads of red chicory, white chicory and / or radicchio, trimmed as necessary and leaves mixed together
a handful *each* of castel franco, Tardivo radicchio leaves, Treviso radicchio leaves and dandelion leaves (add more of one if the others are not available – you just want a good mix of bitter leaves for interest)
120g black seedless grapes, halved
115ml grape or pomegranate molasses
a pinch of dried red chilli flakes
a handful of fresh oregano or marjoram leaves
50ml extra virgin olive oil
bottarga for grating
sea salt and freshly ground black pepper

Preheat the oven to 160°C/Fan 140°C/Gas Mark 3.

While the oven is heating, give all the leaves a good rinse and pat them dry.

Lay half the grapes, cut side up, in a roasting tray. Drizzle with 15ml (a little less than a level tablespoon) of the molasses and season well with salt. Bake for 20 minutes, or until the molasses starts to caramelise and the grapes have shrunk by about one third. Remove from the oven and set aside to cool.

Mix all the salad leaves together with both the fresh and baked grapes, the chilli flakes and half the oregano. Season and mix again.

Whisk the extra virgin olive oil and the remaining 100ml molasses together, then mix into the salad.

Turn the salad into a serving dish, sprinkle with the remaining oregano and grate over bottarga to taste. Serve.

Summer Courgettes

with malloreddus, parmesan and oregano

A vibrant plate of pasta inspired by the frugal cuisine of Sardinia. As is so often the case, a few simple well-chosen ingredients can make for a deliciously satisfying bowl of pasta.

In this recipe the courgettes are carefully fried in olive oil, *fritti*-style, to get a good depth of flavour. I often serve these *fritti* as an accompaniment to meat or fish dishes sprinkled with a squeeze of lemon juice and sea salt.

Malloreddus, or *gnocetti sardinare*, is a small gnocchi-shaped dry pasta from Sardinia, where the water-and-flour pasta is often lightly coloured with a pinch of saffron. If you can't find *malloreddus* then any other small dry pasta shape, such as orzo, will suffice.

Serves 4

360g *malloreddus* or other small
    pasta shape
olive oil
2 large, or 4 small, courgettes,
    trimmed and thickly sliced
2 garlic cloves, crushed
a handful of fresh oregano leaves
finely grated zest and juice of 2
    unwaxed lemons
60g Parmesan cheese, finely grated
50g pine nuts, toasted, for
    sprinkling over
sea salt and freshly ground black
    pepper

Bring a large saucepan of salted water to the boil. Add the pasta and cook according to the packet instructions.

Meanwhile, heat a good splash of olive oil in a deep, non-stick frying pan over a medium heat. When it is hot, add the courgettes and try to spread them out in an even layer over the base of the pan so they cook at the same rate. Leave to fry, unmoved, for 3–4 minutes until the undersides turn golden brown. Flip them over and brown the other sides. Do this in batches, if necessary.

Add the garlic, oregano and lemon zest to the courgettes, and cook for a further minute to lightly cook the garlic.

Drain the pasta, reserving a small ladleful of the cooking water. Add the pasta to the pan, then toss to mix everything together. Sprinkle in half the Parmesan and add the lemon juice, along with some of the pasta water – you might not need it all. Season.

Stir well until the cheese is melted and the 'sauce' is smooth, adding extra pasta water if needed. Divide among bowls and top with the pine nuts and remaining Parmesan sprinkled over. Serve immediately.

Fritto Misto di Pesce
deep-fried seafood

The heart of the *fritto misto* world is to be found in Campania. Fried foods are a speciality of the region – inland you'll find mixed fried meats, olives and vegetables, and on the coast the renowned mixed fried fish. But this is one of those dishes that transcends regionality and all of Italy has created a version of its own. Some versions will just use coarse flour to dust the seafood, while others, like in this recipe, will use a light, veil-like mix not dissimilar to a tempura batter.

The seafood can be whatever you like, but a good selection is important. I have very fond memories of strolling along the promenades of Italian seaside towns with a brown paper cone filled with hot crispy seafood doused in lemon with some mayonnaise to dip the pieces in. Try the fried citrus – I can almost eat a plate of it on its own.

Serves 4

100g plain white flour
2 tablespoons cornflour
125ml chilled sparkling mineral water
rapeseed oil for deep-frying
8 Atlantic prawns, peeled and
   deveined, but with the tail intact
8 small scallops, defrosted if frozen
100g fresh squid tubes, cleaned and
   cut into rings – see page 32, or ask a
   fishmonger to do this
120g fresh sardine fillets (or similar
   oily fish of your choice), skinned
   and cut into strips
4 very thin lemon slices
4 very thin orange slices
a handful of fresh sage leaves
aïoli (page 38 or shop bought), to serve
lemon wedges, to serve
sea salt and freshly ground black
   pepper

Mix together the white flour and cornflour, then whisk in the water to make a batter. Heat enough oil for deep-frying in a deep-fat fryer or heavy-based saucepan until it reaches 190°C. If you don't have a kitchen thermometer, a cube of bread will turn golden in 30 seconds when the oil is hot enough.

Pat the seafood dry with kitchen paper, then season. In batches, dip the seafood and citrus slices into the batter, shaking off excess, and carefully lower into the oil. Deep-fry for 2–3 minutes until golden and crisp. Remove with a slotted spoon, drain on a tray lined with kitchen paper and sprinkle with sea salt. Fry the unbattered sage leaves until crisp, then move to the kitchen paper to drain.

Divide everything among serving plates and serve with the aïoli and lemon wedges.

Spiced Octopus
with pepperonata

Octopus is a stalwart of the Sardinian cooking repertoire and is found in both restaurant and domestic kitchens. Along the coast you'll see octopus divers carefully arranging their catches on the coastal rocks or on extended lines to dry them in the hot Mediterranean sun. In times past, the octopus were beaten on the rocks or rumbled in an arcane salad spinner type device to tenderise the flesh. These traditions have now been largely replaced with modern processing methods.

When sourced and cooked properly octopus is superb. At our restaurants we use large frozen octopus and defrost them very slowly overnight, so the defrosting process tenderises the flesh. If you buy a fresh octopus, freeze it first and then defrost to ensure maximum tenderness. You can also buy excellent pre-cooked octopus imported from Spain and Italy.

The sweet-and-sour braise of peppers along with the sweet and aromatic spices partner deliciously with the rich, charred octopus. Hold on to the Sardinian theme by adding a handful of fresh fennel fronds or fresh dill sprigs just before serving.

Serves 4–6

1 frozen octopus, 1.5–2kg, defrosted
   overnight in a fridge
1 teaspoon ground cinnamon
1 teaspoon coriander seeds, crushed
1 teaspoon fennel seeds, crushed
grated zest and juice of 1
   unwaxed lemon
olive oil
a handful of fennel fronds or
   dill sprigs
sea salt and freshly ground black
   pepper

For the pepperonata
5 large red peppers, quartered and
   deseeded and thinly sliced
2 red onions, thinly sliced
2 garlic cloves, chopped
10 plum vine tomatoes,
   roughly chopped
100ml cabernet sauvigon vinegar
2 tablespoons light demerara sugar
4 fresh thyme sprigs
2 fresh bay leaves

Slice the head off the octopus just above the tentacles and just below the hard, inedible mouthpiece. The head can be discarded. Place the octopus in a steamer pan and steam for 1½ hours, or until very tender. Remove and leave to cool.

Meanwhile, make the pepperonata. Heat a good splash of olive oil in saucepan over a high heat. When it is hot, add the red peppers, onions and garlic, and fry for 20 minutes, stirring as you go. Next add the tomatoes along with the vinegar, sugar, thyme sprigs and bay leaves. Mix everything together, then turn the heat down to medium-low. Continue stirring to avoid catching until the tomatoes cook down into a thick, rich sauce and their natural water evaporates.

Check for seasoning and then remove from the heat to rest. It should have a rich, delicious sweet-and-sour flavour.

Place the spices in a small pan over a medium heat and dry-fry until they are fragrant – be careful, because this will happen quickly – then transfer immediately from the pan to a plate to cool.

Preheat the grill to the maximum heat.

Cut each tentacle into 2 pieces, then rub them with olive oil and season. Grill the tentacles to lightly char and crisp.

Drizzle over lemon juice to taste, sprinkle over the spice mix and then divide among serving plates along with the pepperonata. Finish with the lemon zest and fennel or dill.

Roasted Tuna
with baked tomatoes and basil

Tuna fishing is taken very seriously in Sardinia. The annual Carloforte tuna catch is renowned worldwide and takes place from late April through to early June. The fishermen use the only 'tuna trap' method of fishing still in practice – a method invented by the Arabs in the Middle Ages that uses a series of net trap chambers to catch and haul the fish to the banks of the port. People come from far and wide to see this macabre spectacle and it is considered cruel by some. This technique, however, is more humane than many other modern methods and the catch levels are monitored to ensure there is no overfishing.

This recipe is similar to one that I first tasted in Sardinia – very simple, using the best-quality fish and ripe tomatoes in season. Try to get thick tuna steaks as they will be easier to cook and allow you to achieve a nice crust on the outside and retain a lovely pink colour on the inside.

Serves 4

500g vine tomatoes, cored and cut
   in half widthways
2 garlic cloves, thinly sliced
1 teaspoon coriander seeds,
   lightly crushed
2 tablespoons red wine vinegar,
   such as cabernet sauvignon
olive oil
4 x 200g tuna steaks, each about
   2.5cm thick
leaves from a small bunch of basil
sea salt and freshly ground black
   pepper

Preheat the oven to 190°C/Fan 170°C/Gas Mark 5.

Place the tomatoes in a roasting tray, sprinkle over the garlic, coriander seeds and red wine vinegar, add a good drizzle of olive oil and season well. Transfer to the oven and roast for 25 minutes, or until the tomatoes have started to caramelise and release their natural juices. You'll have a lovely self-made dressing in the pan from the mix of the oil, juices and vinegar. Leave in a warm spot.

Pat the tuna dry, then season each steak with salt and pepper. Heat a good splash of olive oil in large sauté pan over a high heat. When it is hot, add the tuna and fry for 2–3 minutes on each side to achieve a nicely caramelised crust. Remove from the pan if you like your tuna pink inside, but if you want it cooked more, cook it for a further 2–3 minutes, turning it as you go.

Rest the tuna for a few minutes before serving.

Meanwhile, gently stir the basil leaves through the roasted tomatoes. Divide among individual plates, then top each portion with a piece of tuna and spoon over the tomato-vinegar juices. Serve.

Sardinian Fregola
with slow-cooked pork, tomatoes, garlic and fennel

Known as Sardinian couscous, *fregola* lands somewhere between pasta and a grain. It has a lovely nutty flavour and comes in an irregular, rustic shape. Use it as you would pasta, tossed with sauce, or perhaps stirred into long braises as you would a grain to thicken and add bulk. You can toss the *fregola* into salads or simply steam and finish with olive oil to serve as a deliciously simple side dish.

My recipe cooks everything together in a casserole and uses the *fregola* like a nutty pearl barley, similar to a dish I first had in Sardinia. The Sardinian version used wild boar instead of pork. This is a perfect dish to enjoy when you are in need of something robust and comforting.

Serves 4–6

1.2kg boneless pork leg, skin scored
olive oil
6 garlic cloves, crushed and chopped
2 small heads fennel, quartered
3 bay leaves
2 shallots, finely chopped
2 teaspoons fennel seeds
1 tablespoon tomato purée
250ml gutsy red wine, such as
   nero d'avola
peeled zest of ½ unwaxed lemon
8 plum tomatoes, chopped
100ml chicken stock (fresh or
   homemade is best)
130g *fregola*
a handful of fennel or dill fronds
sea salt and freshly ground black
   pepper

A couple of hours before cooking, remove the pork from the fridge, season, rub with olive oil and the garlic. Cover and set aside at room temperature.

Preheat the oven to 150°C/Fan 130°C/Gas Mark 2.

Heat a good splash of olive oil in a large flameproof casserole over a medium heat. When it is hot, sear the pork on all sides to nicely brown. Transfer the pork to a plate and set aside.

Add the fennel pieces to the same pan and brown these all over. Add the bay leaves, shallots and fennel seeds to the casserole, and stir for 3–4 minutes to cook everything down. Add the tomato purée and stir for a minute or so. Return the pork to the casserole along with the wine, lemon zest and the tomatoes. Bring to the boil to reduce the wine and break down the tomato pieces. Pour around the stock and return to the boil again, stirring. Cover and transfer to the oven for 1 hour to cook slowly.

After the pork has been in the oven for 40 minutes, put the *fregola* in a bowl with cold water and leave to soak for 20 minutes, then drain. Sprinkle in the drained *fregola*, pushing it into the stock around the pork. Re-cover and return to the oven and cook for a further 30–35 minutes. The pork should be very soft and tender, and the sauce thickened and rich – the *fregola* will have the texture of cooked pearl barley. If the sauce is too thin or the pork not quite tender, return the casserole to the oven for a further 15 minutes. Set the casserole aside and leave the pork to rest for 20 minutes before stirring in the fennel or dill. Check the seasoning and serve.

Arantzadas

orange and almond sweets

These little delights are typical at Sardinian weddings, christenings and festivals. More of a sweet than a cake and very simple to make, these use the best produce of the region – oranges, honey and almonds, that's all. It's important to cut the strips of orange peel very thin. A citrus peeler, ideal for this job, is a great addition to your kitchen armoury if you don't have one.

I like to add a drizzle of melted dark chocolate, the bitterness of the chocolate cutting through the sweetness of the *arantzada*. Perfect with coffee.

Makes about 30

400g peeled unwaxed orange zest
400g clear honey (traditionally
    lavender is used, but any
    blossom is fine)
400g flaked almonds, lightly toasted
dried unsprayed lavender
    buds (optional)
40g 70% dark chocolate,
    melted (optional)

Ensure all the pith from the orange zest is removed, as it is bitter, then cut the zest into very thin strips (see the introduction, above). Soak the zest in cold water for at least 8 hours, with a couple of water changes. Drain the zest and place on a tea towel to dry well.

Place the honey in a small saucepan over a medium heat. When it is just hot, add the zest, turn the heat down to very low and leave to simmer for 1 hour, stirring once or twice.

Turn off the heat and stir in the almonds. Let the mix cool, thicken and turn sticky before spooning it into individual paper cases. Or you can pour the whole mix onto a greaseproof paper-lined baking sheet and then cut into wedges.

While still soft, sprinkle over the lavender and drizzle over the chocolate if you want. They're ready to serve, but will keep in an airtight container for up to a week.

Panna Cotta
with fruit and amaretto

Panna cotta hails originally from Piedmont, though now it is to be found throughout Italy. My two most memorable panna cotta experiences were firstly in Sardinia at the Osteria del Borgo, where panna cotta has become a signature dish with many exquisite varieties offered. I love their simple vanilla-flecked version served with a seasonal fruit, such as sweet apricots tossed in a little Amaretto. The second great panna cotta experience was in the UK at my favourite restaurant, the River Café, along the Thames in London, where it is served with fresh blackberries and a shot of grappa.

Once you've got the panna cotta technique nailed, the world is your oyster. Here's my favourite version … for the moment.

Serves 4–6

325ml double cream
75g whole milk
70g caster sugar
1 vanilla pod, cut in half with the
    seeds scraped out
2 leaves gelatine, soaked in cold
    water to cover

To serve
100g fresh raspberries, blackberries,
    or strawberries, washed and
    trimmed, if necessary
75ml Amaretto, chilled

Heat the cream, milk and sugar with the vanilla pod and seeds in a saucepan over a medium-high heat until bubbles appear around the surface, stirring to dissolve the sugar. Do not boil. Remove the gelatine from the water and squeeze out any water, then whisk it into the hot milk until fully dissolved.

Pass the mixture through a fine sieve into a jug. Set aside to cool slightly before pouring into individual moulds, glasses or bowls. Transfer to the fridge for at least 2 hours to fully set.

To serve, either turn out the panna cottas onto individual serving plates (dipping the moulds in hot water or blasting quickly with a blowtorch works well), or simply serve in the moulds, glasses or bowls.

Toss the fruit in half the Amaretto and divide among the panna cottas. Pour the remaining Amaretto over the panna cottas at the table.

Index

About the Author

Classically trained with over 20 years' experience, Ben spent his formative career working with Michelin-starred chefs such as Marcus Wareing, Jason Atherton and Stephen Terry at various ground-breaking London restaurants, learning classical techniques along with inspired culinary innovation. He went on to head up his own operations at the Italian restaurant Al Duca in St James, London, and the Crinan Hotel in the West Highlands.

Following this, Ben became chef and partner at Salt Yard Group, where he stayed for 12 years, opening Salt Yard, Dehesa, Opera Tavern and Ember Yard, overseeing the food and menus across the sites. While with Salt Yard, Ben wrote his first book, *Grill, Smoke, BBQ*.

Ben then became the culinary director of Norma on Charlotte Street and The Stafford London in St James, overseeing the food offering throughout the hotel including the Game Bird restaurant, the American bar and private dining. Norma received critical acclaim from the leading UK food critics.

In 2022, Ben became the chef director of Cubitt House, a unique collection of some of the best London pubs, restaurants and boutique hotels.

A regular cookery teacher at some of the UK's leading schools, including Leiths, Divertimenti, Cookhouse at Soho Farmhouse, Chewton Glen cooking school and Bertinet, teaching is one of Ben's passions.

Ben is a regular guest on *Saturday Kitchen*, *Sunday Brunch* and *MasterChef*, and writes for *Delicious*, the *Guardian*, *Telegraph*, *The Times*, *Noble Rot*, *Restaurant* magazine, *Chef* magazine and other publications.

Ben is an accomplished and award-winning food writer, having previously published four cookbooks. *Mediterra* is his fifth book.

Acknowledgements

Nykeeta, my lovely wife, best friend and tiger mum to Piglet and Peanut, our two French bulldogs. Always supportive and critical in all the right ways. Many of the recipes in this book have been honed with her involvement.

My incredibly supportive suppliers who provide the best produce to me and my restaurants: Josh at 2-Serve supplies wonderful, seasonal vegetables and fruit from near and far; Charlie at Walter Rose & Son provides the best meat; Jamie Sinclair at Wright Bros Ltd for spankingly fresh seafood; the team at Belazu for incredible, authentic Mediterranean products I could live on for the rest of my days; Woods Food Service for everything else that's good (and mostly dry); and thanks to Mutti for their home cooking inspiration – canned tomatoes don't get better!

Kris Kirkham, good friend and amazing photographer. This is my fourth book with him, and it's always a joy.

My team at Cubitt House, without whom I could not have put together this book so efficiently while juggling multiple other projects: Richard Sandiford, development chef at Cubitt House (one of the best cooks I know); Neradah Hartnett, executive pastry chef at Cubitt House; Danielle Catano, head chef at the Builders Arms in Chelsea; Mike Lenton, executive chef; and Lewis Hannaford for keeping things ticking along.

Helen Gurnett for offering her time to help with cooking, organising and food styling for the photoshoot. A great partnership! Davina Perkins for the best props and styling.

Jon Croft, Meg Boas, Rowan Yapp, Emily North, Peter Moffat, Shunayna Vaghela and Isobel Turton at Bloomsbury and Bloomsbury Absolute – the best publishing team you could wish for.

Sam and Georgie Pearman, co-chairs at Cubitt House, for the ongoing support and opportunities.

Conversion Table

Liquids

METRIC	IMPERIAL
5ml	1 tsp
15ml	1 tbsp
30ml	2 tbsp or ½fl oz
60ml	4 tbsp or 2fl oz
90ml	6 tbsp or 3fl oz
120ml	8 tbsp or 4fl oz
150ml	¼ pint or 5fl oz
290ml	½ pint or 10fl oz
425ml	¾ pint or 16fl oz
570ml	1 pint or 20fl oz
1 litre	1¾ pints
1.2 litres	2 pints

Length

METRIC	IMPERIAL
5mm	¼in
1cm	½in
2cm	¾in
2.5cm	1in
5cm	2in
10cm	4in
15cm	6in
20cm	8in
30cm	12in

Weights

METRIC	IMPERIAL
15g	½oz
20g	¾oz
30g	1oz
55g	2oz
85g	3oz
110g	4oz / ¼lb
140g	5oz
170g	6oz
200g	7oz
225g	8oz / ½lb
255g	9oz
285g	10oz
310g	11oz
340g	12oz / ¾lb
370g	13oz
400g	14oz
425g	15oz
450g	16oz / 1lb
1kg	2lb 3oz
1.5kg	3lb 5oz
2.5kg	4lb 8oz